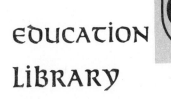

Windmills, Bridges, & Old Machines

OTHER BOOKS BY DAVID WEITZMAN

Traces of the Past
A Field Guide to Industrial Archaeology

Underfoot
An Everyday Guide to Exploring the American Past

My Backyard History Book

Windmills, Bridges, & Old Machines

Discovering Our Industrial Past

DAVID WEITZMAN

Charles Scribner's Sons | New York

Charles Scribner's Sons
Macmillan Publishing Company
866 Third Avenue, New York, NY 10022
Collier Macmillan Canada, Inc.

Printed in the United States of America

First Edition

5 7 9 11 13 15 17 19 20 18 16 14 12 10 8 6 4

Library of Congress Cataloging in Publication Data
Weitzman, David L.
   Windmills, bridges, and old machines.
   Includes index.
   Summary: A guide to the study of America's
industrial past through examination of early
engines, furnaces, locomotives, windmills,
foundries, canals, bridges, and other
industrial antiquities.
   1. Windmills—History—Juvenile literature.
2. Bridges—History—Juvenile literature.
3. Machinery—History—Juvenile literature.
[1. Industrial archaeology. 2. Archaeology.
3. Windmills—History. 4. Bridges—History.
5. Machinery—History] I. Title.
TJ823.W455   620'.00973   82-3231
   ISBN 0-684-17456-1   AACR2

Contents

Two centuries of American Transportation history side-by-side along the Chesapeake & Ohio Canal at Georgetown, Washington, D.C. Drivers caught in rush hour traffic probably found themselves wishing that Canal Clipper II *were in service again and wondering if canal boats are such an old-fashioned idea after all.*

Introduction

We're about to take a walk in time, back through the years when America was growing. Along the way we'll be looking for the work of some of America's first builders and engineers, two centuries of canals, windmills and waterwheels, steam engines and bridges, furnaces and foundries and locomotives, all kinds of wondrous things. We'll learn how they work and how they changed our lives. After a while, when we've visited many places, we'll begin on our own to piece together the story of Americans at work. The search needn't take us very far. We're sure to find something close by . . .

just around the corner,

A gasholder house, built in 1873, still stands on a street in Troy, New York. Inside was once a huge iron tank that held gas used in nearby houses for lighting, cooking, and heating.

downtown,

The "El," Chicago's elevated railway, travels high above traffic in the downtown streets on the Union Loop, a system of riveted steel girders supporting tracks and stations (1892).

or just a little farther
along a bike trail.

Carrick Furnace at Metal, Pennsylvania (1825)

Some things we wish we could see again
have been gone a long time, remembered
now only as faded images in tattered
and yellowed photographs.

Others remain—
abandoned,
desolate mysteries . . .

Chicago, Burlington and Quincy Railroad roundhouse, Guernsey,
Wyoming

needing our imaginations to bring back the action, sounds, and smells of another time.

Union Pacific roundhouse, Ogden, Utah

At some of the places along our way we'll meet interesting people—the miller down at the old windmill; Richard Lewes, the iron-master; Peter Cooper, who's building a locomotive; molders; stone masons; bridge builders; engineers; surveyors—working people, who built a nation and ran its machines.

For some things we'll have to look hard . . .

Wendel Bollman's wonderful iron bridges, built for the
Baltimore & Ohio Railroad, were thought to have
disappeared long ago. Then this one, built in 1869, was
discovered in the thick brush of the Little Patuxent River
near Savage, Maryland.

but for others
we'll only need
to look again.

Smithfield Street Bridge, Pittsburgh, Pennsylvania (1883). A beautiful example of the lenticular or parabolic trusses designed by Gustav Lindenthal. This is the oldest known steel truss bridge in the United States.

We'll find a lot from this century,
the working places of your
grandparents and great-grandparents,
and a few sites that go back
to America's very beginnings. . . .

Republic Steel furnace,
Cleveland, Ohio.

Hook Windmill, East Hampton, Long Island, New York (1806, restored in 1939).

Flour from Wind

Your first glimpse of a weathered, brown shingle windmill flying lacy wood-lattice wings will be reward enough for even the most tiring history walk. Part of the surprise is discovering that there are windmills in America. You've probably guessed that they go back a long way. If something about these unusual six- and eight-sided structures tells you they must also have come from somewhere far away, you're right there, too. The idea of the windmill came to America from Holland with the first Dutch settlers, back in the early 1600s. Today, most of the surviving windmills are to be found where the Dutch first settled. And that makes them doubly interesting to historians. They tell us part of the story of how the first immigrants made their daily bread and cereal. They are wonderful machines and fine examples of the carpenter's craft. And they stand as markers of early Dutch settlements.

Windmills were already centuries old in Holland and England—all over the world, in fact—when they came to America. As in the old country they were put to all kinds of work, grinding grains, pumping water up out of wells and off of marsh lands, powdering rock into plaster, and running sawmills. Another of the earliest uses of the windmill was harvesting salt. Windmills pumped sea water up onto land walled all around by earth dikes. The sun would evaporate the water, leaving white salt caked to the soil. The salt would be scraped up with wide, flat wooden shovels and then sold in nearby towns. The very first windmills ran saws to cut the timbers and boards the settlers would need for houses and barns. None of these earliest windmills has survived, but old drawings of New Amsterdam—as the Dutch called their colony along both sides of the Hudson River in what is now part of New Jersey, and Manhattan and Long Island, New York—show them dotting the landscape. A Dutch immigrant wrote home, "As we sailed into the harbor the horizon was pierced by scores of windmills, taller than any we have seen elsewhere."

The Dutch and English immigrants' choice of the windmill for power, then, was partly custom. It was one of the many proven ideas brought from Europe

Murphy's Mill, San Francisco, California (1905). The wooden support on the back of the cap is all that remains of the fantail that once forced the sails into the wind.

and made to work in America. But windmills also made good sense. There were few good streams to provide water power in areas where mills were needed. The winds off the ocean, however, would fill windmill sails all year round. They would still be spinning when mill ponds, races, and waterwheels jammed with ice during the harsh winters.

Windmills made sense elsewhere, too, and you'll find them—not many, mind you—scattered throughout the country. As a child in Illinois, I used to visit the Heideman Mill near Addison, built in 1867. As an adult, I found to my surprise that there are windmills in California. Murphy's Mill, one of two built in 1905 to pump well water for San Francisco's Golden Gate Park, stands today, its stilled and battered lattice sails facing into the gusty winds coming off the Pacific Ocean.

2

No matter where you find them, though, remember that windmills may also be markers. Here may be the last remains of a vanished ethnic community. What's the origin of the town's name? What about the names of the oldest streets or the oldest businesses in town? And the old timers—where did their immigrant ancestors come from? England, Holland? (The names and birthplaces on the oldest stones in the cemetery are also a good clue.)

Chances are, the mill you've found no longer runs. Most were abandoned years ago when steam engines, then electric motors and big city mills took over their work. Still, with a little imagination—your historical imagination—the old mill will run for you again. The white sails will billow and flap in the wind. There! The long vanes are whirling, blurring high above your head. Swish, swish, swish, swish . . . like a giant pinwheel. The creaking of old machinery comes from inside. A voice is calling to you over the whirlwind. It's the miller, there in the doorway, beckoning you inside, to return with him to the 1700s. . . .

An eight-sided room! (That's the way windmills were usually built, and in a few minutes you'll see why.) The ground floor is stacked to the floor above with sacks of grain and flour, bushel baskets of dried corn, and bags of freshly ground corn meal. "Watch out," the miller cautions. A sack of flour descends from a hole above to the floor with a thump. Each timber in the place vibrates with a pleasant throbbing, rumbling, chattering coming from somewhere overhead. Following the miller up the tight, narrow stairs to the second floor, you see where it's coming from.

Every corner, the entire space from wall to wall and from floor to ceiling, moves with spinning gears, cog wheels, wallowers, pulleys, and shafts. Two immense stones turn in the middle of all this. It's like being inside some enormous clock made all of wood. Flour dust dances in the shafts of sunlight streaming through the wavy panes of glass. The air is heavy with the smell of fresh flour and candle wax. The sounds are the creaking of wooden machinery and the gritty rubbing of heavy millstones five feet across, turning one upon the other.

"The one on the floor is called the 'bed stone,'" the miller says loudly above the clacking of wooden cogs against wooden wallower gears. "It's stationary. The one on top that's turning we call the 'runner stone.' It's driven by that vertical main shaft there that goes up into the top of the mill." Your eyes follow the turning main shaft—a foot thick and made from a tree trunk—up to where it passes through the great spur wheel. Off the great spur wheel come cog

3

Wooden wallower gear in the Van Wyck-Lefferts Tide Mill near Huntington, Long Island, New York (c. 1795).

wheels, pulleys, and belts driving other machines, a screener and a bolter, and the sack hoist.

"When the grain or corn comes in," the miller explains, "we put it through the screener. The screens let the grains of wheat or kernels of corn through but keep out leaves and twigs, stalks and stones that might have gotten in. The screened grain goes into this funnel-shaped hopper above the runner stone . . . here, I'll put some in. See how it goes down into the hole in the center of the runner stone?" Fresh flour begins coming out from between the stones and collects in the wooden vat at the base. Some of the flour is fine, some of it coarser.

"Now we'll put this through the bolter," the miller says, taking a bucket of flour from under the meal spout. "Inside the bolter the flour sifts down through pieces of cloth. The cloth lets the fine flour pass through but holds back the coarser stuff, the middlings." The miller collects the middlings and puts them into the hopper once again. "One more time through and it'll be pretty fine."

4

The miller's helper scoops flour into sacks and sews them closed with a big needle and coarse thread.

"Too fast, she's too fast," the miller shouts and suddenly bounds up another flight of stairs. Running up behind him, you find yourself at the top of the mill, inside the cap. The little space is filled with the biggest gear wheel you've ever seen, turning on a squared shaft. It's sixteen feet across! But the strenuous struggle and grunts of the miller distract you from the spinning wheel. He needs you to pull while he pushes on a large handle. "This is the brake," he shouts between tugs on the handle. "We're tightening an iron band around the brake wheel to slow it down." Sure enough, with both of you working, the clak, clak, clak, clak of the wooden teeth against the wallower gets slower and slower.

"Whew! Got to talking to you there and didn't notice the machinery speeding up. Well, we're here. The brake wheel is attached to the inside end of the

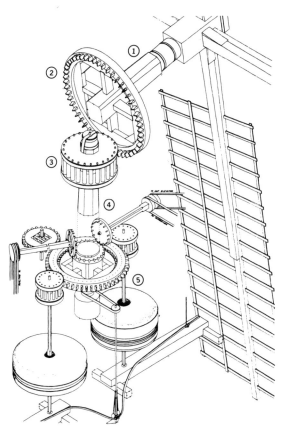

This isometric drawing lets you look through the walls and floors of the Hook Windmill and see how the machinery is arranged inside the building. All the parts—windshaft (1), brake wheel (2), wallower (3), main shaft (4), and great spur wheel (5)—are made of wood.

windshaft. The outside end has the vanes and sails on it. And that big wallower is on the upper end of the main shaft you saw turning the running stone below." The miller reaches for a wooden paddle in a bucket, pulls out a glob of waxy tallow, and smears it inside the wallower teeth. Wax. Tallow. That's what you smelled: not candles, but tallow used to lubricate where the wooden parts rub together (and for candles, too). All the moving parts of this mill are made of hardwood. Even the bearings are hardwood. "You must be careful," the miller warns. "This whole mill's filled with wooden parts rubbing against one another. I've seen it happen, and it's a sorry sight for a miller to see. Let a part go without tallow and it'll heat up so hot it'll burst into flames and set the whole mill afire."

Running a mill, you've begun to realize, isn't as simple as it looks. The gentle breeze turning the sails could, within just a few minutes, turn into a storm. "What do you do then?"

"Well, if the wind's up just a bit," the miller answers, "we'd come down on the brake just like we did. But then I'd watch it really carefully. If the wind starts to blowing, really blowing, I'd tighten the brake till the whole thing stops. Then you and I and my apprentice there would be really busy for a while. We'd climb up the sail bars as fast as we could and furl the sails. Otherwise those sails would get to going so fast we'd never be able to stop them. Tear the whole mill apart, they would. I've seen that happen, too. You know, we're the weathervane for the folks all around," the miller says, laughing. "The sailors and fishermen hereabouts keep an eye on the windmill. If they don't see any sails out, they don't go out. And if they see us clambering up the sail like the devil's after us and bringing the sails in, they know a storm's brewing and it's time for them to come in, too."

Clunk! Clak, clak, clak, clunk! Suddenly the room is turning. Everything's going around: the gears, the cap, everything. The top of the mill is revolving around. There, it did it again!

"It does that every now and then," the miller says, laughing at the look on your face. "Let's go downstairs, outside, and I'll show you why."

Outside, away from the mill and looking up toward where the miller's finger is pointing, you see a little windmill on the side of the cap opposite the big one. "Now, that's called a fantail. When the wind shifts, the fantail starts to spinning and turns some gears inside the mill. See, there it goes again. The

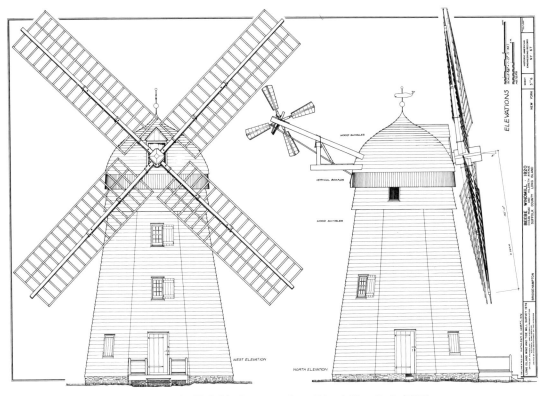

The Beebe Windmill, Bridgehampton, Long Island, New York (1820).

gears turn the cap of the mill around so that the sails are always hard into the wind, no matter which way the wind blows. That's a pretty new idea. The first mill I ever worked in—that's a long time ago—we had to go up into the top and turn a capstan that moved the cap around. That was hard work, I'll tell you. Back a long time before that, windmills had a pole—a 'tail pole' they called it—that reached from the cap down to the ground. The miller and his helpers would come out and push with all their might against the lower end and force the sails around into the wind again."

Now you realize why the mill is shaped that way. The cap of the mill, and with it the windshaft and sails, can be turned all the way around. "And that's why the windshaft and sails are tilted up at an angle like that," the miller points

7

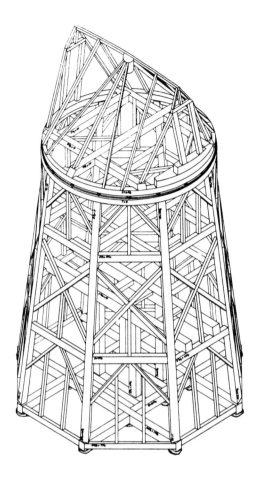

The artist has taken the siding off the Hook Windmill, East Hampton, Long Island, New York (1806), to show us how the carpenters framed the building with heavy timbers. You can see how the cap is built separately so that it can turn all the way around the mill.

out. "The sails catch the wind a bit better at that angle and the sails more easily clear the sides of the mill."

Well, you've discovered today what exciting machines windmills are, but still they seem cumbersome and tricky to run. It's getting late, but there's one last question. "Don't you wish sometimes, when the wind just won't blow, that you had a steam engine?" The puzzled, questioning look on the miller's face makes you realize suddenly that you've asked the wrong question at the wrong time. It's time to be going on your way . . . back to the twentieth century.

Waterwheels and Sawmills 2

Windmills are more spectacular, but most of our power throughout the 1600s, 1700s, and well into the 1800s came from waterwheels. There were thousands of them all over the country. Most of them are gone now, but the Mill Creeks and Miller Falls that run through just about every town in America remind us they were once there.

Four different kinds of waterwheels were used—overshot, pitchback, breastshot, and undershot—and in some parts of the country you'll be able to find one of each easily. These drawings from Oliver Evans's *The Young Millwright and Miller's Guide,* printed in 1795, will help you identify wheels you find. Evans invented many improvements for flour mills, and you'll be hearing more about him a little later.

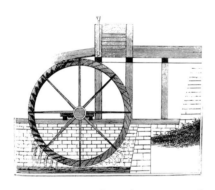

The millwright's choice of one or another kind of wheel depended on how much water there was and its head (how far it fell). If the head of water was ten feet or more, the millwright would usually choose to build an overshot wheel. Water is brought to the top of the wheel by a flume or sluice. The wheel is turned by the weight of the water filling several buckets. Wheels might be built wider to hold more water, and sometimes two or more wheels might be mounted on the same main shaft.

Pitchback wheels revolve in the opposite direction because the water strikes the back of the wheel. All millers had arguments for their favorite kinds of wheel, and those who liked pitchback wheels said the water left the buckets faster and didn't slow the upward motion of the wheel.

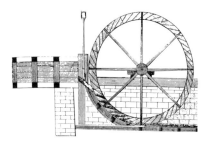

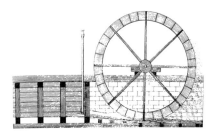

If the millwright had a lower head of water than he needed for an overshot wheel, say, six to ten feet, then the breastshot wheel would be his choice. If you count them you'll see that fewer of the buckets are full at one time in a breastshot wheel. Because of this, breastshot wheels were made wider than overshot wheels so that each bucket held more water.

Where there was no head of water or just a couple of feet, an undershot wheel would be used. You'll notice that the undershot wheel has no buckets; instead, there are paddles called "floats." That's because an undershot wheel doesn't hold water like the others but moves with the water flowing under it. For an undershot wheel to work well, there has to be a lot of swiftly flowing water going under it.

To appreciate how wonderful wind- and water-powered sawmills must have seemed back in those days, you need to know how sawing was done by hand. Much of the sawing was ripping a timber down its full length to make boards. The timber would be laid across a deep pit in the ground. Then the top sawyer would stand on the timber and the pitman would climb down into the pit. Each grabbed onto the end of a long saw and began sawing. The top sawyer pulled up and the pitman pulled down; up and down, up and down, it went until the cut was finished. The top sawyer guided the saw along a line chalked down the log, and the pitman, well, he got a face full of sawdust every stroke. (By the way, if your name is Pitman or Sawyer it's very possible your ancestors took their names from doing this kind of work.)

Windmills and water-powered mills were often built with both milling and sawing machinery inside. Since you neither sawed wood nor ground flour all the time, you could get more use out of the mill. The saw was attached to the main shaft or wind shaft by a couple of cranks that changed the turning motion of the shaft into an up-and-down motion for the saw. Not surprisingly, these were known as up-and-down mills.

An alert archaeologist can tell what kind of saw was used to cut old wood and even date the structure with this clue. While you're exploring an old barn,

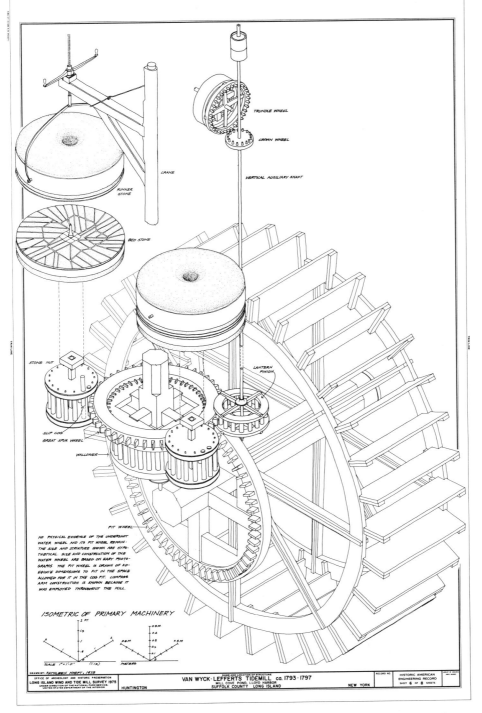

The undershot wheel and machinery of Van Wyck–Lefferts Tide Mill near Huntington, Long Island, New York. The mill was built about 1795, and its machinery, too, is all made of wood.

Iron overshot waterwheel at Thomas Shepherd's Gristmill in Shepherdstown, West Virginia. The mill was built in 1734; the 40-foot wheel was installed in the early 1890s.

house, shop, or wooden truss, look closely at the saw marks on the timbers and boards. Here's what to look for:

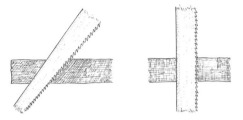

Because the top sawyer and pitman held their saw at an angle, pit-sawn timbers will have diagonal, unevenly spaced saw marks. Most timbers were sawn this way up until the early 1700s.

Evenly spaced, vertical saw marks are the mark of an up-and-down mill. This is the kind of saw you'd find inside early windmills and water-powered mills, and some were even run later with steam engines. Up-and-down mills were in use from the early 1700s through the early 1800s.

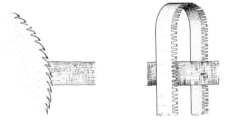

The first circular sawmill was built about 1814 and very soon after that replaced the up-and-down saw at big mills. Circular saws were faster and could be run directly by a windmill, waterwheel, or steam engine without the need for cranks. The circular saw blade runs truer and wastes less wood than the up-and-down saw that wobbled in the middle and made a thicker kerf. Circular saws were also more portable and continue in use right up to the present in small logging operations.

Since about 1850 larger mills have been using huge bandsaws. Bandsaws are made by cutting teeth into one side of a flexible steel belt and then welding the ends together to make a continuous band. Modern bandsaws run so fast and the wood feeds into the saw so smoothly that you probably won't be able to see any saw marks at all.

13

Lift lock gates over a century old, like these near Augusta, Georgia, are still to be found along America's old canals. The Augusta Canal, built in the 1840s, began here at the Savannah River. The same water that moved boats through the nine-mile canal also ran the waterwheels powering cotton mills along the way.

Along Old Towpaths 3

A canal is a great find for a young historian. It can be explored at length on foot, bicycle, or with an adult in a canoe or rowboat. And canals are not hard to find once you know where to look. Hundreds of miles of canals have been built all over the country; many were used in this century, a few to this day. Everything's right out there in the open for you to see. You'll find locks made of cut stone, wooden lock gates that still work, small dams still keeping water levels up, bridges (some of the oldest in America), and, maybe, a gatekeeper's house. Just around the bend, where a weathered schoolhouse is all that remains of an old town, there's a plank landing. Wait there at the landing for a while and you might catch a ride on a packet, one of the low, flat-bottomed boats that carried passengers, goods, and mail up and down the canal. But you won't need your historical imagination this time. Several packets have been restored or rebuilt from the original plans and are operated by canal historical societies. These groups of volunteer historians work to restore and keep up canal structures, too. In some places they've restored whole sections, miles of canals (and they'd welcome you as a member to help).

Canals are more than just ditches filled with water for boats. There's a lot of civil engineering to be learned here and a lot of history as well. Walking a deserted, deeply worn towpath or gliding smoothly on the quiet water, it's hard to imagine how busy this scene once was. Dozens of boats might go by every hour, stacked with firewood, logs lashed together, barges heaped with coal or grain, packets carrying passengers, freight boats with decks piled high with barrels or teeming with livestock, fishermen in small boats, kids swimming or just sitting on the banks watching, waving to packet passengers, and teams of horses and mules on the towpaths tugging at the long lines to the boats. If it's occurred to you that canals were America's first interstate highways, you wouldn't be far off. They were that and every bit as important to our life in those days. When the system was begun in the late 1700s and early 1800s it was the largest engineering project ever in America (still impressive, even alongside

15

The passing of a canal packet was good reason to stop work in the fields or to walk along the banks on the way home from school. The crowd gathered along the tow path of the Ohio and Erie Canal to watch and wave to the freight boat St. Helena II *gliding by behind a team of mules reminds us what life along the canals might have been well over a century ago. The* St. Helena II *was built in 1970 by members of historical groups at Canal Fulton, Ohio.*

all our accomplishments since then). And reflected in these quiet waters is one of the most exciting chapters in our history.

Back in the 1700s there was no way to haul heavy, bulky goods like cotton bales or iron ore long distances overland. There wasn't any need to. The large cities grew up on the Atlantic coast or inland along large rivers, easily reached by boat. Each city was a market center for the many small towns and farms clustered nearby, and hauling could be done by wagon or up and down the river. America, at this time, was a narrow strip along the Atlantic seaboard not reaching very far inland. But most important, there wasn't a lot of movement of goods from one colony to another or, later, between states. In fact, that was discouraged. High taxes on goods brought in from another state kept them out, protecting local merchants and manufacturers. Americans didn't need things brought from another state anyway; each city, town, village, and farmstead was self-sufficient. There were no huge factories making clothes and furniture to be shipped all over the country because, well, you made your own clothes and your own furniture. Or you got them in trade with a neighbor. There was a cabinet-maker in town, as well as a blacksmith, and a wagon maker, and a miller, a sawyer, and anyone else you might need. Then, sometime in the 1780s or 1790s, this began to change.

What happened was complicated. (History, as you've guessed by now, is never simple.) But, somehow, canals both caused it to happen and came about because it was already happening! Merchants and factory owners began to look for markets in other states. The few canals already in operation showed them that this was possible. And by building a canal from, say, Baltimore to Harrisburg, you could "capture" that market, make sure your goods were bought because only your goods could get there. New York didn't buy coal from Pennsylvania because it was cheaper to ship it all the way from England! But, people began to wonder, what if there were a system of canals connecting Pennsylvania with New York, New Jersey, Maryland, and beyond? Questions like that were being asked all over the country, and the answer was a system of canals that would help make a nation out of separate states.

Canal builders chose routes that included navigable waterways like large rivers and lakes in the system. The Erie Canal, for instance, made it possible to travel or ship goods by boat all the way from New York City, north to Albany, west to Buffalo on Lake Erie, and, then, across the lake to Ohio and Michigan. The Wabash & Erie and Miami & Erie canals connected Lake Erie with the Ohio River, which ran to the Mississippi River. Once you had reached Toledo, then, Indiana, Illinois, Missouri, Kentucky—the entire Mississippi Valley— was open to travel, and it was all made possible by canals.

Not all the shipping was east to west, of course. You can see how the canal system connecting rivers and lakes would encourage the growth of cities inland. It was easier to ship now, faster and therefore less expensive. Before the Erie Canal was completed in 1825 it cost about twenty cents a mile to ship a ton of freight overland from Buffalo to New York City. By canal it would eventually cost less than a penny! Almost anything could be shipped now, and was. Tobacco and cotton from the South moved north along the Mississippi and eventually to markets in Illinois and Ohio. Grain, cattle, and hogs moved along rivers and canals to Chicago, turning the city into a market for grain and meat packer for a nation . . .

Hog Butcher for the World,
Tool Maker, Stacker of Wheat,

17

poet Carl Sandburg named the city. Sugar from Puerto Rico, unloaded on New York docks, sweetened cakes and cookies in St. Louis, Missouri, and life along the Santa Fe and Cimarron Trails.

The canal you've found, then, was built to connect two cities, two rivers, lakes and rivers, or several cities and towns along the way. It had a historical direction that explains why it was built. That's obvious if you're standing at one end of the canal or the other, but it may not be if the part of the canal you've found is somewhere in the middle. Though a canal runs both ways, it appeared to run one way or the other depending on where you were standing in the 1840s. Using your historical imagination, you might want to stand there for a moment. As an inland factory owner, for example, you might see the canal flowing away from you, carrying your products out toward a river, then to an ocean port and, perhaps, to some country around the world. If the other end of the canal is in the Pennsylvania coal fields, you'd think of it coming toward you, bringing coal to fuel the steam engines running your factory or sugar mill. As a shop owner in a city at one end of a canal that has its other end at port, you see the canal flowing toward you bringing wooden crates of imported glassware and bolts of wool cloth to sell to your customers. To an immigrant, just arrived in New York or Baltimore or some other Atlantic port, the canals all seem to flow westward, to a place on the American plains you would call home.

Oh, Susanna!
Don't you cry for me;
I'm a-going to Indiana
With my banjo on my knee.

There's a chapter in your history textbook titled "The Westward Movement," "Westward Ho!", or something like that. It probably mentions canals, especially the Erie Canal, and only briefly. What you remember of that chapter are the wagon trains of settlers and their belongings winding up the eastern slopes and inching over the passes of the Appalachian Mountains. Wagons carried a lot of settlers to the new territories, all right. And wagon making too, is an important chapter in the history of early American technology. But that's what wagons did, inch along. And they couldn't carry much either, not when compared to a canal boat. You might get a few tons in a wagon and consider ten miles a darn good day's travel. But a single canal boat could carry thirty or forty tons and make fifty, eighty, a hundred miles in a day. If your family settled originally in the Great Lakes states and the Mississippi Valley it's more likely they came by canal boat than by wagon.

Canal and lake boats brought the populations of whole cities and states to the plains. The arrival of boatload after boatload of immigrants at Atlantic ports seemed to hurry along the work of canal building. Once open, the canals then attracted more and more immigrants. What happened is to be seen in the census figures from those days. There were about 350,000 people in Indiana in 1830. Two years later work began on a canal that would bring settlers in from Toledo at the west end of Lake Erie. In 1840 Indiana's population was 684,000. The work of canal building continued throughout the 1830s and 1840s, and in 1850 the population of Indiana was 988,000! In that same time the population of Illinois went from 157,000 to 851,000. "All the immigrants from the East came in by the canal," an early settler in Indiana told a historian. "The boats would take grain to Toledo and bring back immigrants and their goods by the hundred."

It must have been exciting to live by a canal in those days, walking the tow paths. An article in an Albany, New York, newspaper reported boatloads of Swiss immigrants passing through. The new Americans stood on the deck, catching their first glimpses of their adopted homeland still dressed as they were then they'd left Switzerland. They had brought with them their wagons, and plows and tools. They must have continued on to Lake Erie, then south on the Miami & Erie Canal to Cincinnati on the Ohio River. If you put your finger on a map at Cincinnati and trace the Ohio south about fifty miles, you'll find a city they founded and settled. Vevay, Indiana (named for Vevey on Lake Geneva in Switzerland) is still there in Switzerland County. "Almost every summer day in the latter 1830s and 40s," a Pennsylvania newspaper reported, "groups of merry German immigrants in wooden shoes might be seen on the decks of line boats going west from Harrisburg towards Ohio, Indiana and Illinois." (Line boats, by the way, were slower and more crowded than the packets, and less expensive, which is why they were preferred by immigrants. Line boat fare was 1½ cents a mile; packets charged about 5 cents a mile.) So by canal came the original members of the German communities in Cincinnati, Chicago, St. Louis, Milwaukee, and Indianapolis, and dozens of other nationalities came as well. Perhaps your great-great-grandparents were among them.

Time and the forest have all but hidden Lift Lock 1 on the Great Falls Canal in Fairfax County, Virginia (1797). The canal was begun in 1785 under the direction of General George Washington.

Building a Canal 4

It's impossible for us to imagine, in this day of giant earth-moving machines, how much work there was to building a canal in the early 1800s. Mountains of earth, rock, and clay had to be shoveled and blasted and hauled away to make the channel, or prism, as it was called. Miles and miles of rivers had to be dredged deeper and widened. Whole forests of trees had to be felled and then whole forests of stumps cleared. Thousands upon thousands of stone blocks had to be chiseled from solid rock, hauled to the work site, lifted into place. Thousands of workers working hundreds of thousands of hours, the countless shovelfuls, strikes of the pick, blows of the hammer, the hauling, sawing, lifting, chopping, digging, prying, drilling, tightening, leveling, scraping . . . all by hand.

The wonder of it all is that the work did not take decades or generations or centuries, only years. The numbers make it look so simple. In one decade, the 1820s, over 800 miles of canals were opened in New York, Pennsylvania, Delaware, and Maryland. Thirteen hundred more miles of canals were being built and nearing completion. The 364 miles of the Erie Canal were completed between 1817 and 1825. When you visit a canal you'll realize, too, that these weren't just little ditches. A typical canal prism might be fifty feet wide and ten feet or more deep.

Long before the digging could begin, a route would have to be surveyed and mapped. Little of the countryside had been mapped then. Much of the country had not even been traveled! The few maps available told nothing about changes in elevation—distances up and down—or the depth of a river or the amount of water in the channel from one season to the next. Falls might be shown on a rough map, but how high were they? All of this would have to be found out before engineers could even begin designing the many structures that make up a canal.

Oh yes, there was another problem. America had no engineers. Two of the

21

earliest canals, begun in the 1790s, had been built by an English and a Swedish engineer. But the great works of canal building in the next three decades, including the Erie Canal, would be done without engineers. If that seems a serious problem to us now, it doesn't seem to have bothered anyone then. After all, there was a job to do: a nation needed canals. Even if there were no university-trained engineers, by gum, it would get done anyway.

As it turned out, there was a fine engineering school in America; it was called the Erie Canal. John Jervis was one of the graduates of the Erie Canal "school." He started out as an axeman, clearing paths through the forest for the teams surveying the canal's route. Two years later he was appointed an "engineer." Later he built other canals as the chief engineer and built railroads as well. Still later in his career he designed and built the Croton Aqueduct, including high masonry bridges, which he had never done before.

James Geddes and Benjamin Wright were also graduates of the Erie Canal school of engineering—they built it. They surveyed the route, directed the design of all the structures, and supervised the building of the canal. Both were lawyers when they took on the job, with but a little surveying experience. Nathan S. Roberts, another "amateur," designed locks with a greater lift than any in use at the time. And Canvass White, another student at the Erie school, discovered hydraulic cement, cement that would harden under water. By the way, with the exception of Canvass White, none of these men had ever seen a major canal!

If these early canal builders weren't quite engineers, they were certainly much more than surveyors. They were given complete responsibility. The canal company's charter might simply call for "a canal between Huntsville and Indian Creek," or "from Hennepin on the Illinois River to Watertown, Illinois, on the Mississippi." Nothing more. The surveyors' task was to find the best route, design the structures, hire crews, organize work schedules, arrange deliveries of materials, supervise the work, look after countless details. Today, a similar project would be done by dozens of contractors and subcontractors.

The work began with the survey, when teams of surveyors and their assistants would set out on horseback in search of a route. Months, years were spent in the wilderness. Hundreds of details needed to be thought about at one time: the lay of the land, water, the amount of rock that would have to be removed, whether this point along the bank or that point over there was the best site for a bridge, how far the quarry stones would have to be moved, how they would be hauled, how much forest would have to be cleared. And, of course, there was a budget to keep within. The teams might have to go the length of the proposed route a number of times, backtracking, trying new routes, until they had the right one. Finally, the team returned with their measurements, records, sketches, and maps.

One of the drawings the engineers will make from their measurements in the field is a profile. A profile is a kind of side view or section drawing of the route surveyed. Here's how the land might have looked.

And here's the engineer's profile of the route.

The engineer's not concerned about small changes in elevation; the canal prism is about ten feet deep and will even them out. But larger changes are a problem. And this is where the detailed work of designing the canal begins.

A canal must be kept full of water. That's obvious enough, but not as easy as it sounds. Water is brought to the canal through feeder channels from nearby, rivers, streams, and lakes (though some feeder channels might have to be twenty or thirty miles long). When the canal is full—usually four to seven feet deep—the water must flow from one end to the other slowly and without any sudden rapids or falls. So the entire canal must be almost level. Almost. If the prism is level, the water won't flow in the right direction or at all. And if the canal prism slopes too much, the water runs too swiftly, making it hard for the mules and horses to pull the heavy boats upstream. The bed of the Erie Canal was so carefully dug that there was a fall of only one inch every mile!

To keep a canal level while it's flowing up and down hills would seem to call for a magician rather than an engineer. Actually, it is done with a kind of magic, the canal lock. Locks are easily understood if you think of them as a flight of water stairs going up a hill or down, if you're going that way (they work both ways). Instead of having the water and canal boats run downhill, the engineer puts in a lock or flight of locks that "step" the boat along with the water down the slope. You'll find many locks along your canal walk, maybe several in just a few minutes' walking distance. Some have been restored and operate just as they did back in the early 1800s. Groups like the American Canal Society, the Illinois Canal Society, and others, whose members are historians like you, do this kind of work. But most of the locks you'll find will have some parts missing, making it difficult to understand just how they work. Let's imagine we're on a canal packet, approaching those locks back in the days when they were operating.

The lock is marked by the lockkeeper's house of stone up ahead on the right. He lives there and tends to his locks during the daylight hours. Most canals prohibited traffic after dark (except on moonlit nights), and on some the Sabbath was strictly observed.

The mule driver and steersman work carefully now to ease the huge packet into the lock. (There's a fine for bumping the gates.)

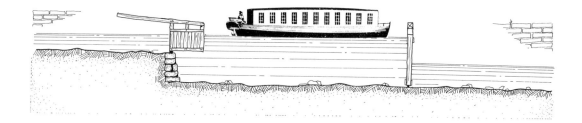

When the boat is inside the lock, the crew swings the upper swing gates closed by pushing and pulling on the balance beam. Some lockkeepers hung wooden boxes filled with stones from the ends of the balance beams to make the gates easier to open and close.

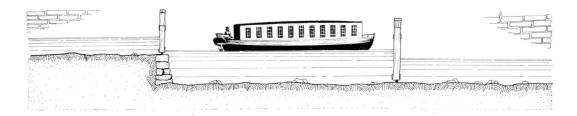

By now—it takes longer to tell about it than do it—the lockkeeper has opened up the wicket gates and the water in the lock has begun flowing out into the lower part of the canal. As the water level in the lock falls, the boat is lowered until . . .

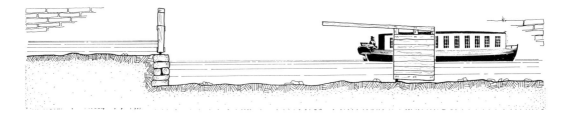

it reaches the lower level of the canal. Once the lower swing gates have been opened, the packet could continue on its way. If another boat were waiting to go in the opposite direction, it could enter the lower part of the lock as soon as your boat cleared the lower gates.

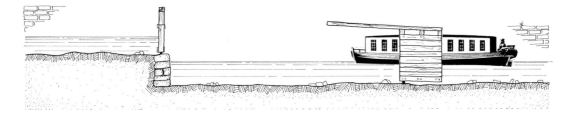

When the packet was inside the lock, the lower gates would be closed . . .

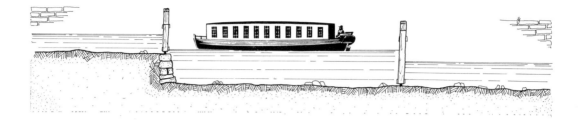

and the lockkeeper would open the filling ports to let in water from above, raising the water level in the lock and the packet boat . . .

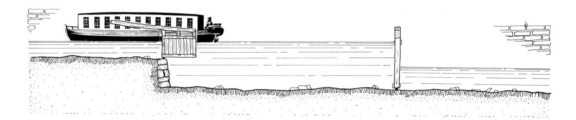

to the upper level of the canal.

At really steep places along the canal a flight of several locks would be needed. The convenient pound reach—the distance a boat could be raised and lowered—for the early canals was figured at five or six feet. Later the pound reach was increased to ten or twelve feet and even eighteen feet. Raising and lowering boats more than ten feet, then, usually required another lock. These flights of locks work the same way as the single lock your packet went through

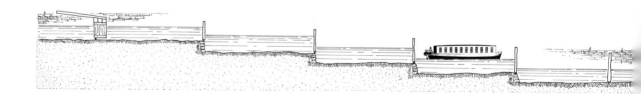

. . . except that boats could be raised and lowered greater distances (and you'd have more swing gates to open and close). At one place on the Erie Canal, above Troy, New York, boats moved up and down through sixteen locks in just three miles. At Lockport, engineer Nathan S. Roberts solved the waiting problem and also built the first locks with a twelve-foot lift. Movement through several locks slows traffic going in both directions, and boats piled up at each end of the locks waiting to go through. Roberts had two flights of locks, five locks in each flight, cut side by side out of solid rock. One flight lifted ascending boats to the upper level of the canal. And at the same time, boats going the other way could descend down through the other flight.

Now, perhaps you've discovered the magic of the lock. All this lifting and lowering of boats usually weighing sixty tons and more is done without any machinery. The hardest work at the lock is swinging the gates open and closed. The quiet waters of the canal do all the rest.

F. B. Tower.

W. Bennett, sc.

CROTON AQUEDUCT AT YONKERS.

Lith. J. A. Brown & Co. 87 Nassau St. N.Y.

For D. T. Valentine's Manual 1862

HIGH BRIDGE DURING CONSTRUCTION OF THE LARGE MAIN
Viewed from the West Gate House looking East

Water for a City 5

Cities never seem to have enough water these days. But, then, there's nothing new about that. Back around 1800 there were already a few large cities in America, and already water was a problem. American cities at that time weren't the largest in the world, not by any means. They were, however, growing at a much faster rate than cities elsewhere. Between 1800 and 1850 the population of some European cities doubled; a few even tripled. Yet during that same fifty-

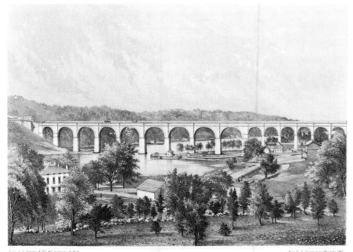

HIGH BRIDGE DURING CONSTRUCTION OF THE LARGE MAIN
Viewed from the Westchester side looking North-West

Old drawings and paintings tell us a lot about early American engineering. In fact, hand-drawn images are our only glimpses into the time before the use of photography was widespread. These old drawings show us the early American landscape around the Croton Aqueduct, Yonkers, New York, and what the aqueduct structures looked like when they were being built in the mid-1800s.

29

year period the population of Philadelphia increased four times, Boston's five times, and New York City's more than ten times. That's right. In 1800 the population of New York City was about 64,000. The census of 1850 counted 696,000.

American cities grew up in a single lifetime. Let's imagine that you were born in the little settlement around Fort Dearborn, on the southwest shore of Lake Michigan, around 1816. So few people lived there that no one bothered counting, but it might have been a couple hundred. By the time you were celebrating your thirty-fourth birthday you would be living in the city of Chicago with 30,000 other people. Your child's thirty-fourth birthday (you'd be sixty-eight) would be celebrated in a city of 503,000. And the Chicago in which your grandchildren grew up would have a population of nearly two million! It all happened in about three generations, or about eighty years.

No one planned it that way. The mayor and his council didn't come together, deliberate, and announce at the next town meeting, "Hey, we're going to build a city here with two million people." No one could have even envisioned such growth. Cities . . . just happened. It might begin at a natural port on the ocean, on the shores of a sheltered bay, by a good boat landing on the river, at a trailhead, near an iron field or granite quarry, at the crossroads, where the canal ends. At first there are just a few families. Others come, and now there's a village, a community with a school, a church, a smithy, and farm work to be done. Farm workers come from all around and the village becomes a town. Then, one day, the railroad track crews or canal builders arrive, some with their families. A generation or two pass and hundreds, thousands, tens of thousands, hundreds of thousands, millions of immigrants and big city people from the East get off the trains and packet boats.

And you've got a water problem (to say nothing of a few others). At first, a well dug near each house did fine. Some folks just went down to the creek and returned with all the water they needed in buckets. Later on the mayor might call everyone together to build a wooden tank up on the hill just outside of town. It's kept filled by a spring or water run through a flume from a nearby lake or river. Suddenly, there just isn't enough water.

That's what happened to New York City. By 1800 there were 50,000 people living in the City, making it the second largest in the United States (Philadelphia, with 81,000, was the largest). Already there was a serious shortage of drinking water. The Hudson, East, and Harlem Rivers surrounding Manhattan Island were salty from mingling with the Atlantic tides. The Island is almost everywhere solid rock, and the few wells, ponds, and springs that gave water to the first settlers were no longer enough. The only safe drinking water came from springs in New Jersey brought across the Hudson in the barrels of water boats. And there was dangerously little water for firefighting in a city of wooden buildings. Within a few years two great fires threatened the City. And in 1832 an epidemic of cholera—a disease carried in bad water—killed 3500 people.

So New York City began looking elsewhere for water, to the fresh water in the rivers up north, particularly the Croton River. Here was a river with a heavy, constant flow and enough water to supply the City's needs and then some. About forty million gallons of water flowed down the river each day, more than four times what the City would need. The only problem was it was thirty-five miles away!

The job of bringing the water to the City over that distance was given to John Jervis. John had finished elementary school, become a surveyor's assistant and, later, engineered the Erie and the Delaware and Hudson Canals. John's idea was, first, to dam the Croton River, making a reservoir holding 500,000,000 gallons of water. Then, to carry up to 35,000,000 gallons of water a day down to the City, he designed a marvelous aqueduct.

A long aqueduct like the Old Croton is actually many different kinds of structures. A few are hiding. The original dam and gatehouse appear only now and then during droughts. When the rainfall is normal they're under about forty feet of water held by a higher dam built more recently. You may be able to visit parts of the sixteen tunnels—the Old Croton was closed down in 1968—though most of us will see them in the section drawings. But, fortunately, much of the genius of John Jervis and the work of some 5000 laborers recruited off ships arriving from England and Ireland remains.

Most impressive are the massive embankments that carried the water in a stone pipe or conduit high across wide valleys. Brooks, creeks, streams, rivers, roads, and, at one place, a wooden bridge to a water-powered mill, pass under the embankments through 114 culverts. Some are small, about six feet by six feet. Then the conduit passes over Sing-Sing Kill (and a modern road) on an eighty-eight-foot stone arch. Finally, Croton River water makes a spectacular entrance into the City, crossing the Harlem River on a 138-foot high stone

The Old Croton Dam just after it was completed. Since this dam is now deep under the water held by an even higher dam, this little drawing is especially valuable to historians.

bridge supported by sixteen towering piers and gracefully turned arches.

The opening of the Croton Aqueduct was celebrated with marching bands, parades, church bells, and cannon fire on July 4, 1842. That morning John Jervis and his engineers opened valves that let water into the huge reservoir that would hold 150 million gallons. (But it's not there anymore; the New York Public Library stands there now.) Caught up in the excitement of the day, the Mayor of New York City promised the crowd that "pure and wholesome water will be our legacy to countless generations into the future." But it didn't quite work out that way.

About thirty years after the completion of the aqueduct the population of the City went over one million. And since most of them now considered indoor flush toilets and bathtubs and kitchen sinks a necessity, a larger New Croton aqueduct was put into service. Today, two more aqueducts—the Delaware and Catskill Systems—have been added to the Croton System. New Yorkers draw water from eighteen reservoirs and four man-made lakes. And at last count they were using over a billion gallons a day!

Steam

6

The history of steam engines in America began in Pittsburgh in 1809. That's when Oliver Evans, a mechanic and millwright, built the first steam-driven flour mill. Evans didn't invent the steam engine. The first practical engines had been built by Thomas Newcomen in England a century earlier. But Evans spent a lot of time studying Newcomen's engine, thinking about steam engines and thinking, too, about all kinds of ways to put them to work. He experimented with a steam carriage and built an immense steam-dredging machine for deepening canals and rivers. The 40,000-pound paddle-wheel boat on wheels propelled itself out of the shop, around the corner, down the street, and right into the river! But it was Evans's steam-powered flour mill that touched our imagination. Within a few years, steam engines were doing America's work, from crushing sugarcane on Louisiana plantations to weaving cloth in New England textile mills, and driving saw- and gristmills everywhere in between.

Portable engines like these brought steam power to the American farm. The early engines were moved around by teams of horses and hooked up to threshing machines, bailers, flour mills, and other farm machinery. Later they could move about on their own and could be used for plowing. In 1800 it took a farmer 56 hours of hard work to grow an acre of wheat. In 1900, using steam engines like these, it took only 15 hours!

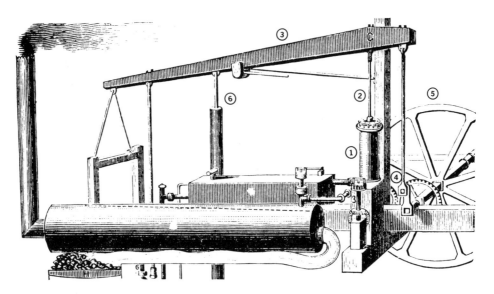

Oliver Evans's Columbian steam engine. Steam rushes into the cylinder (1) and pushes up on the piston, piston rod (2), and beam (3). As the beam moves upward it turns the crank (4) and the heavy flywheel (5). The turning flywheel and crank pull the beam down, returning the piston to the bottom of the cylinder. Another burst of steam sends the beam up again. The rod (6), moving up and down with the beam, opens and closes a valve that lets steam into the cylinder at just the right time. This is called a single-acting engine because the steam pushes only one way.

Before steam engines, work was done a number of ways. Waterwheels and windmills, as we've seen, did the heavy work. Machine tools—lathes, drill presses, and saws—were powered with foot treadles like old sewing machines you may have seen. Horses and mules going around in circles turned other machines. But all these methods had limitations. When the parts to be machined got big, really big, like huge castings for locomotives, foot treadle power just wasn't enough, no matter how furiously the machinist's assistant might pedal. Waterwheels are powerful enough, but they stop when the creek freezes over in the winter or slows to a trickle in a drought. What's more, factories and shops had always to be built next to streams and rivers, or have the water brought to them by expensive canals and flumes. The steam engine could turn out steady power almost anywhere and at any time and ran on the cheapest fuel there was, wood.

When Evans put a steam engine to work in a flour mill, other people began thinking of ways to use steam power. Eli Whitney's cotton gin, for instance. Before Eli's invention, workers combed and picked seed from cotton by hand. A worker hand-cranking, pedaling, or pumping up and down on the footboard of a cotton gin could clean forty pounds of cotton a day. That was something in the late 1700s. Later, when horses were harnessed to larger gins, the output went up to 400 pounds a day, and that was really something in those days. Then, in the 1830s, iron works in the South began making steam engines for sugar mills and cotton gins. Now three workers tending the engine and a larger version of Eli's gin could clean in a single day anywhere from a thousand to over 4000 pounds of cotton!

The steam engines used in mills, factories, and gins are called stationary engines. That's because they're bolted down to a foundation (and because later on "portable" engines that could be hauled around were built on runners or wheels). The earliest of these were beam engines, the most wonderful engines

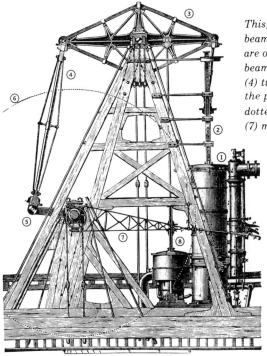

This, as you might guess, is called an A-frame beam engine. The cylinder (1) and piston rod (2) are on the right side of the engine. As the iron beam (3) moves up and down a connecting rod (4) turns the crank (5). The artist has removed the paddle wheel so you can see the engine, and a dotted line (6) shows where it would be. The arm (7) moves the valve rod (8) up and down.

of all to watch. Everything is in motion. Long, slender rods dip in and out following the measured up-and-down rocking of a giant beam balanced on a tall iron column. Cranks spin, polished brass fly-ball governors whirl, and a massive flywheel turns slowly, slowly, slowly as though it weighed ounces instead of tons. Beautiful designs cast into the ironwork and a bright coat of paint made each engine special. You wonder how any work got done around such a machine. The temptation, it seems, would be to sit and watch it for hours.

Beam engines were expensive to build and affordable only by large factories. In the 1820s lighter, simpler engines appeared that could be used in small mills and shops. These engines were "direct acting." The piston rod was connected directly to the crank through a connecting rod, saving all the space taken up by the beam of a beam engine. Direct-acting engines could be made to go faster, too.

Direct-acting engines could be either "vertical" or "horizontal." The piston in a vertical engine moves up and down in a vertical cylinder, turning the crank from above. The piston on a horizontal engine moves back and forth in a horizontal cylinder, turning the crank from the side. Vertical engines take up less floor space and can fit into a small workshop or even a small boat. Actually,

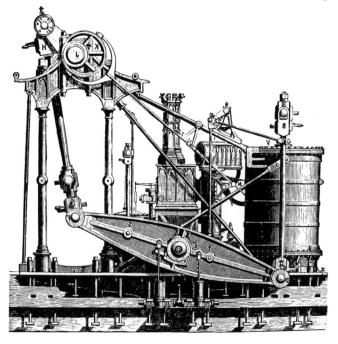

Imagine all those rods and levers and cranks in motion as smoke puffs out of the cast-iron medieval castle! This is a side-lever engine that was used on a ship. Lowering the overhead beam to the side permitted the engine to sit lower in the bottom of the ship, making it ride in the water better.

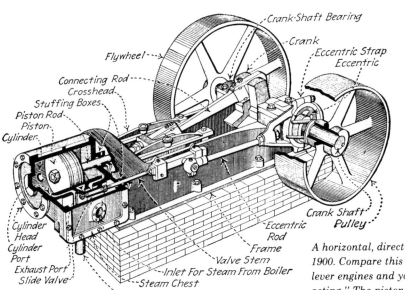

Crank-Shaft Bearing

Crank

Eccentric Strap
Eccentric

Flywheel

Connecting Rod
Crosshead
Stuffing Boxes
Piston Rod
Piston
Cylinder

Cylinder
Head
Cylinder
Port
Exhaust Port
Slide Valve

Eccentric
Rod
Frame
Valve Stem
Inlet For Steam From Boiler
Steam Chest
Steam Outlet (Exhaust)

Crank Shaft
Pulley

A horizontal, direct-acting steam engine from about 1900. Compare this engine with the beam and side-lever engines and you'll see why it's called "direct acting." The piston and piston rod are connected directly to the crank with a connecting rod. The cylinder of this engine is double acting. Steam is let in on both sides of the piston by a slide valve so that the piston pushes and pulls on the crank.

engineers liked vertical engines for another reason. If you look at the section drawing of the horizontal engine, and think about it, you'll realize that all the weight of the piston—a large heavy iron disc—rests on the bottom of the cylinder. When the piston moves back and forth in the cylinder there's more friction on the bottom of the piston and cylinder than on the top. Over the years of use this causes the cylinder and piston to wear unevenly. Perhaps now you can understand why an engineer designing a very large steam engine would prefer a vertical design.

By the late 1800s almost every pulley, gear, wheel, and axle that turned in America was turned by steam. Engines became more efficient. Compound engines with two and three cylinders were built to use the steam two or three times before it was exhausted. And, probably, not even Oliver Evans could have envisioned how monstrous steam engines could get. A beam engine built by George Corliss for the 1876 Centennial celebration stood forty feet tall. The cylinders were almost four feet in diameter and the stroke of the piston was ten feet. The engine weighed 700 tons and developed 1500 horsepower. At the Centennial celebration the engine ran 8000 machines in Machinery Hall, but similar engines in waterworks all over the country pumped millions of gallons of water in a single day!

37

Little Engines 7

If you're wishing you had been born a hundred years ago, just so you could run a steam engine, there's no need for that. There are several thousand steam engines around today that you can run yourself. They're not to be found in old factories and mills, but in toy stores, hobby shops, museums, school science labs, and, maybe, in your grandparents' attic. They're toys, of course, but they run exactly like the real ones (except that you won't need a ton of coal).

Toy steam engines have a long history. In fact, many of the builders of the first steam engines built model engines to try out their ideas. Later, the first toy engines sold in stores were replicas of these inventors' models and some of the engines actually in use. Since steam engines were first built in England, that's where toy engines first appeared. Over the years several magazines have been published for model engineers, and at least one of them is available today. The English still make toy steam engines, and you'll also find engines made in the United States and Germany.

What's interesting also about toy steam engines is that they're probably the only toy made today that was made a century ago. What's more, they've changed very little over that time. Some engines made today have electric coils for heating the boiler, but so did toy engines made in Germany and England a century ago. The engines you see in stores are not much different from those your grandparents or great-grandparents might have played with when they were children. You should ask them if they remember playing with toy steam engines; one may even be stored in the attic. Toy engines were once used for demonstrations in science classes. If you're going to an old school you might ask the science teacher if there's a toy steam engine hiding out in the back of a cabinet or up on a dusty top shelf in the storeroom. Restoring the engine and getting it running again would be a good science project (and one other students would appreciate).

Toy steam engines in the Montgomery Ward mail order catalog of 1895.

The joy of engines to generations of children is their realism. If you've run a toy steam engine, you've run a real steam engine. Everything's there, the fire-box, boiler, safety valve, whistle, stack, throttle valve, cylinder, piston, connecting rod, crank, and flywheel. Some toy steam plants come with two engines that run off a larger boiler. Some have reverse gear, and most manufacturers also make a small dynamo that will generate enough electricity to light a flashlight lamp. You can also buy a complete machine shop to run with your engine—shaper, milling machine, table saw, drill press, forging hammer—all run off of a line shaft as they would have been in a factory years ago. Some engines come as kits you can build yourself. But most toy engines are easy to take apart, revealing the secrets of the piston inside the cylinder and the little slide valves.

Mamod Minor No. 1, miniature of a portable steam engine (English).

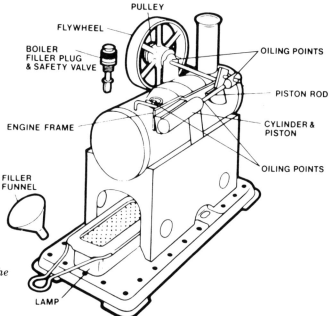

The parts and oiling points of the Mamod Minor No. 1 (English), a toy "portable" with the engine mounted on the boiler.

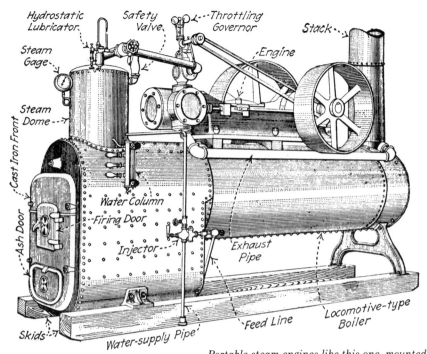

Hydrostatic Lubricator · Safety Valve · Throttling Governor · Stack · · Steam Gage · Engine · Steam Dome · · · Cast Iron Front · Ash Door · Water Column · Firing Door · Injector · · · Exhaust Pipe · Skids · · Water-supply Pipe · Feed Line · Locomotive-type Boiler

Portable steam engines like this one, mounted on skids, could be moved around and used on farms, at construction sites, and on docks to load ships. This is the kind of engine the Mamod Minor No. 1 is modeled after.

Here are some simple instructions for restoring and running a little engine.

1. Engineers took a lot of pride in their machines and were always careful to keep them oiled, clean, and shiny. Each time you run your engine you'll want to make sure it's well lubricated. Oiling slows wear, protects the metal parts from rust and corrosion, and makes everything run smoothly. Use the same oil your parents use in their car, which is probably 30W or 10-40W (and don't use light sewing machine or household oil). You'll need a little oiling can or a toothpick to drip oil into the oiling points. Oil all the bearings, the holes in which shafts turn. You won't need much; a drop or two will do it. Then oil the cylinder. Oil here makes a seal between the piston and the cylinder wall so that steam can't leak out past the piston. And keep a small rag in the back pocket of your overalls to catch drips of oil and water.

2. The first step will be to fill the boiler with water. On a real steam engine an injector pumps a constant supply of water into the boiler. But you'll have to

41

unscrew the boiler filling plug and then fill the boiler with a little funnel. If you fill the boiler with hot water you'll get up steam faster and you'll get a longer run with a fueling. It's important not to overfill the boiler, because there must be a steam space above the water. Since you can't see into the boiler, engines have water-level guages. Little engines usually have an overflow plug at one end of the boiler that tells you when there's enough water. Some engines have a glass window in the end of the boiler so that you can actually see the level.

3. Little engines, like real ones, have safety valves. The "pop valve" pops open if the pressure in the boiler gets too high. The pop valve is built into the filler plug of most engines. If you've found an old engine and are running it for the first time, make sure the safety valve works. Hold the filler cap between your fingers and push on the spring that fits down into the boiler. If it moves in and out smoothly and freely, the valve is working. But if it's stuck, you must

free it before running your engine. Oil it and work it back and forth until it works smoothly.

4. Little engines use one of three kinds of fuel. Some have electric heating elements in the firebox and you just plug them in. Some have a small alcohol burner with a handle. (It will be packed with what looks like cotton and have a screenlike cover.) And some have just a small tray that holds solid fuel tablets. Boxes of tablets are inexpensive (you'll get a box with a new engine) and can be found at hobby shops and toy stores. You'll find alcohol at the drugstore, but make sure it's "denatured alcohol." Rubbing alcohol contains water and doesn't heat as well. The tablets and alcohol light easily with a match and burn cleanly. If you're running an old electric steam engine you've found in the attic for the first time, ask someone to check the wiring and connections to make certain they're safe.

5. You'll have steam in three to four minutes, so stand by the throttle valve. Before starting the engine, give a couple of pulls on the whistle chord to warn everyone that you are starting up and to stand clear of the engine and machinery. Open the throttle and give the flywheel a spin. You can use the throttle to adjust the speed or stop the engine.

6. When the alcohol burner or solid fuel goes out, the boiler will be nearly empty. Be sure to refill the boiler each time you refuel. After the last run, take off the filler plug for a while and let the boiler dry out. Electric engines will have a water gauge or a water-level glass. Keep an eye on your gauge to make sure there's a safe level of water in the boiler whenever the engine's running. **43**

Nassawango Iron Furnace, Worchester County, Maryland (1830–1849). The observant historian will notice the heat exchanger on top of the furnace, coils of iron pipe through which the blast passed before going down through the tuyeres and into the furnace.

Making Iron at Bear Creek 8

Scattered about the countryside, sometimes deep in the forest almost overgrown by trees and brush, are hundreds of mysterious stone pyramids. Maybe you've seen one. Most have sloping sides, tapering toward the top, each with an arched opening. Some are round; a couple have been found with three sides; a few have six or eight sides. They're thirty, forty, fifty feet tall. Some are made of carefully cut stone neatly laid in even courses one upon the other. Others are more rustic, made of rocks gathered from nearby or even rough logs, squared and notched. And they're all alike somehow, as though they were all meant for the same thing.

What on earth could they be? They sit unnoticed, miles from the nearest town. Their isolation, that's the puzzler. Nothing around to give even the smallest clue as to what they are. Certainly there's nothing about them to even suggest that they were part of one of America's earliest and most important industries. These silent stones are actually old blast furnaces. From their hearths flowed millions of tons of iron to make our first axes, tools, plows, locomotive parts, bridge members, cannon, steam engines, nails, hardware, cooking pots, everything we would need.

The furnace was the heart of the ironworks. Inside its thick walls the iron was smelted, melted away from the rock in which it is found. Iron is plentiful in the earth, and much of it is close enough to the surface to be dug up. The problem is that iron doesn't come out of the ground as big chunks of metal. It's mixed in with rock and clay and other minerals; so to get pure iron you have to first crush the iron-bearing rock, the ore, into small pieces. Then the ore is heated in a furnace of burning charcoal until the iron melts, separates from the rock, and trickles down through the charcoal to collect in the bottom of the furnace, in the hearth. It sounds simple, but there's a lot of work to making iron and a lot of skill needed each step along the way to make good iron.

But why was such an important industry out in the wilderness? You'd

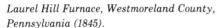

Laurel Hill Furnace, Westmoreland County, Pennsylvania (1845).

Ross Furnace, Westmoreland County, Pennsylvania (1815).

expect ironworks to be close to factories in large cities. Remember that in the early 1800s there was no way to ship bulky, heavy stuff long distances over land. A large furnace might burn 5000 or 6000 cords of wood in the eight or nine months it was in blast every year (a cord of wood is a stack four feet wide by four feet high by eight feet long). And it took two or three tons of ore to make one ton of iron. It simply made better sense in those days to put the ironworks near the raw materials. The finished iron, cast in small bars called "pigs," could be hauled out more easily than millions of tons of raw materials could be hauled in. Later, iron ore and coal would move all over the country on canal and river barges, Great Lakes ore boats, and long trains of hopper cars. But, until then, furnaces were built close to iron ore deposits and great forests. And that's where you'll find them today.

When you come upon an old stone blast furnace it's hard to imagine what went on there. Usually, too little is left of an ironworks to even guess how it worked. From the drawing of Buckeye Furnace you can see why. The casting shed, engine house, and bridge house were all built of wood. Over the years numerous ironworks—some as old as 200 years—have weathered away, burned, or been torn down. Trees and grass have grown up in the casting bed. Foundation stones, even the furnace stones, have been carried away for other building work. What remains, then, is anything stone or iron, the furnace, stone buildings and crumbled foundations and maybe a heat exchanger, some lengths of iron pipe or the rusted parts of a blast engine. But that's where the fun and the work of archaeology begin.

46

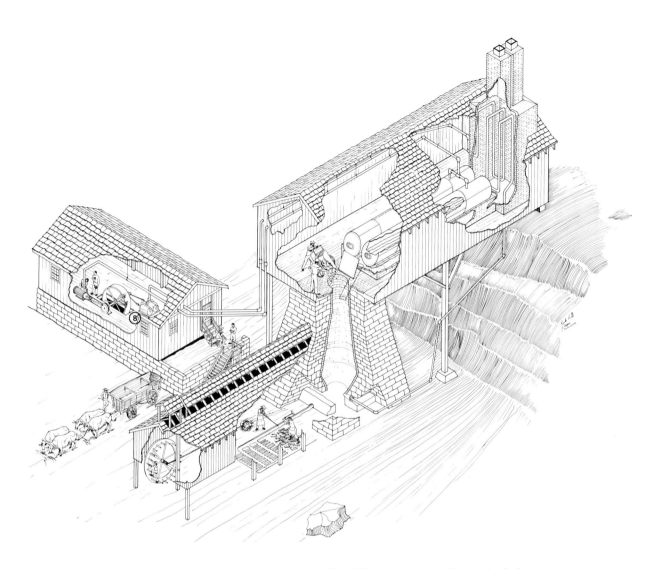

Buckeye Furnace (1851–1894) near Wellston, Ohio. Fillers dump a wheelbarrow load of ore into the furnace. Below, in the casting shed, a molder tends to the pouring of pigs while a helper uses a sledge hammer to separate cooled pigs, and another operates a human-powered winch to drag away a heavy chunk of slag. Just outside the casting shed a teamster awaits a load of pigs with his cart and two yoke of oxen. At Buckeye the furnace heat is used before it exhausts up the stacks. First, it passes under two boilers making steam for the steam engine driving the blast machines (upper left). Then the hot gases pass through a heat exchanger in the brick stacks which heats the blast on its way to the tuyeres in the tuyere arch at the base of the furnace. Buckeye Furnace remained in blast twenty-four hours a day for nine months each year.

The remains of one of the oldest iron furnaces in the South, in Bartow County, Georgia. Mark A. Cooper started making iron here in the 1830s and operated this furnace until it was destroyed in the Civil War.

Take a walk around the furnace. Look into the arches. You might be able to look up into the furnace from the hearth and see what's left of the fire-brick lining. Be sure to notice the stonework. Old ironmasters were as proud of their furnaces as an architect would be of a fine house. A lot of care went into setting the stones and turning each arch. In front of the work arch—the largest of them—you might still see traces of the casting bed. Feel the ground there and see if it's sandy. Then, find a shady spot close by. Sit down and let your imagination drift back to sometime around the 1840s. . . .

The air fills with the furnace roar and shimmers with the heat of tons of red-hot charcoal. Smoke, and now and then bright balls of flame, burst skyward from the top of the furnace and gritty cinders rain down all around you.

"More coal, Marcus, and another barrow of limestone as well." A figure has stepped from the dark of the work arch out into the early evening sun and shouts instructions up to the two men working at the top of the furnace. It's Richard Lewes, the ironmaster here at Bear Creek Furnace. His father, grandfather, and a great-grandfather were ironmasters back in Wales. "Tom, are the molders finished yet?" He calls out now to the men working in the sand of the casting shed. "The iron'll be let out soon, within this hour. Be ready there, lads." And almost as quickly as he appeared the busy ironmaster disappears back into the smoky dark.

Marcus George is one of several free black men who work at the furnace. He, too, is the third generation of ironworkers in his family, born here in the little settlement that surrounds the furnace. Marcus and his crew of fillers have been tending to their fire for almost twelve hours now, since six o'clock this morning. After their pour this evening they'll have a night's rest and another crew will take over and be ready to pour at six tomorrow morning. That's the way it goes here at Bear Creek, day after day, week after week for eight or nine months. Then, the furnace will be "blown out," and needed repairs done to the fire-brick lining and machinery.

Making iron is a lot of work for a lot of people. The ore must be dug out of the ground with the picks and shovels and the energy of hundreds of men (another thirty years will pass before Bear Creek gets its first steam shovel). Meanwhile another large crew digs limestone out of a nearby hillside. Still another crew fells acres of trees and cuts them into lengths with axes. Cartloads of wood are hauled by oxen to the charcoal pits. Here it will be tightly stacked into neat piles by the colliers, covered with a layer of dried leaves and another layer of soil. A fire is set under the pile and left to smolder for four or five days. When the covering of soil is removed a warm heap of charcoal stands ready to be delivered to Marcus's crew at the furnace head. At some larger ironworks charcoal is made in large stone ovens or kilns, but here at Bear Creek Furnace it's been done this way for as long as anyone can remember.

All of these workers and their families lived together in a small town—sometimes as many as 500 or 600 people in all—clustered around the furnace. Most of them worked at ironmaking: woodcutters, colliers, miners, molders, founders, patternmakers, and all their helpers and apprentices. Since they lived in a community surrounded by wilderness the services of others would be needed, too: carpenters, company clerks, teamsters, wheelwrights, blacksmiths, farmers, weavers, bakers, and cooks. Bear Creek was a town of houses, barns, stores, boarding houses, schools, workshops, and churches like any other American community. Sadly, it would take a whole team of experienced archaeologists to find even a trace of it now.

"You can come up here if you want to." Marcus is calling to you. "Climb   **49**

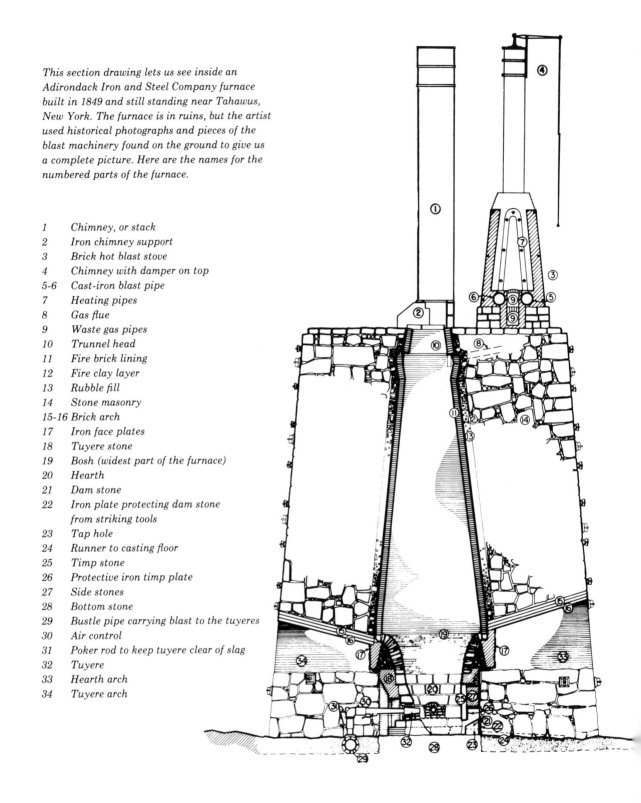

This section drawing lets us see inside an
Adirondack Iron and Steel Company furnace
built in 1849 and still standing near Tahawus,
New York. The furnace is in ruins, but the artist
used historical photographs and pieces of the
blast machinery found on the ground to give us
a complete picture. Here are the names for the
numbered parts of the furnace.

1   Chimney, or stack
2   Iron chimney support
3   Brick hot blast stove
4   Chimney with damper on top
5-6 Cast-iron blast pipe
7   Heating pipes
8   Gas flue
9   Waste gas pipes
10   Trunnel head
11   Fire brick lining
12   Fire clay layer
13   Rubble fill
14   Stone masonry
15-16 Brick arch
17   Iron face plates
18   Tuyere stone
19   Bosh (widest part of the furnace)
20   Hearth
21   Dam stone
22   Iron plate protecting dam stone
     from striking tools
23   Tap hole
24   Runner to casting floor
25   Timp stone
26   Protective iron timp plate
27   Side stones
28   Bottom stone
29   Bustle pipe carrying blast to the tuyeres
30   Air control
31   Poker rod to keep tuyere clear of slag
32   Tuyere
33   Hearth arch
34   Tuyere arch

up the hill there and cross over the bridge to the top of the furnace here." Go ahead.

"Watch out there, lad. Let that barrow of charcoal by. And you don't want to get too close to the furnace head either. It's nearly 3000 degrees in there!" The fillers begin bringing wheelbarrow after wheelbarrow of white stone up to the furnace head and dump it in. Marcus has been asked the question enough times to know that you're wondering what the rock is for. "It's limestone. Iron-workers call it 'flux.' The limestone helps the iron flow out of the rock and sand and all, down through the coal. . . ." WHOOMP! WHOOMP! Marcus's explanation is drowned out by a tremendous roar and explosions of blue flame, smoke, and cinders out of the furnace. "That's why it's called a 'blast' furnace," one of the fillers calls out. "If you go down and find the ironmaster you'll find out what happened."

Wandering around the base of the furnace, you see a bustle of activity in one of the smaller arches. "Give me a hand here, boy." It's the ironmaster struggling with a nozzle attached to an iron pipe coming out of the ground and pointed into the red-hot furnace. Together you wrestle it into position. "There. Now it's putting the blast where we want it," the ironmaster says, wiping the sweat off his face with his neckerchief. "Those nozzles—there are three of them—are called 'tuyeres' [say *tweers*]. They put the blast right in where it's needed. Over in the shed, on the other side of the furnace, is a steam engine driving two blast engines. The air goes up pipes to a heat exchanger up where the fillers are working. There it's heated by the hot gases coming off the burning

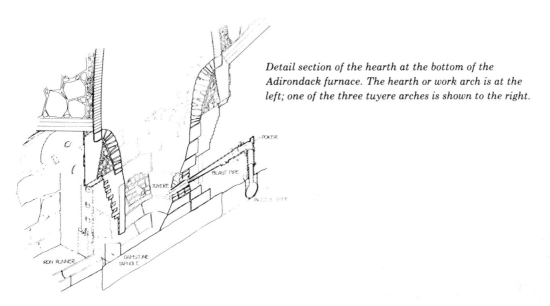

Detail section of the hearth at the bottom of the Adirondack furnace. The hearth or work arch is at the left; one of the three tuyere arches is shown to the right.

charcoal and then it comes down here to the tuyeres. You ever blow on a fire to make it hotter? Well, that's what the blast does. Gets a lot of air moving through the powdery charcoal and ore, gets it good and hot. Here, come with me. I'm needed at the hearth."

The work arch is the hottest place you've ever been. The ironmaster peers through a small hole into a pool of fiery orange molten iron. His face glows in the hot light. "Hand me that long skimmer there, boy." He reaches the long iron bar into the hole and pulls out a blob of glowing cinders. Fairy wand sparks shoot off the cinders and bounce crazily off the walls of the arch. "This is slag, dirt and rock that stays on top of the iron in the hearth. The limestone holds it all together, makes it easier to get out." Now's the time to ask the ironmaster the question that's been on your mind for a while now, the one about why all the charcoal and limestone and ore don't just fall down into the hearth.

"That's a good question, boy. If you could see into the furnace you'd see that the walls slope inward very steeply just above the hearth. That's the boshes. The furnace burden packs against them and can't fall down. You're a

This old charcoal oven and the remnants of furnaces and foundry mark the site of Old Irontown, near Cedar City, Utah. English, Scots, and Welsh miners and ironmakers started up the iron works in 1868 with nearby iron ore deposits.

bright fellow asking questions like that, but you'd best get out of here. There's going to be hot iron all over in just a minute."

You've noticed for the first time now the pattern of channels cut in the sand floor. A stone "iron runner" leads from the hearth to the beginning of the runner. "You see," Tom the molder explains, "the channels carry the iron to these molds we made in the sand. We just put a wooden pattern in the sand, pack the sand tight around it, and pull it out, leaving a little trough there. Each one of these fills up with iron and becomes a pig. That's the way iron is sold, in pigs. Makes it easy for the foundryman to handle . . . oh-oh, watch out, the ironmaster's getting ready to let the iron out."

The ironmaster takes another long rod with a pointed end and picks carefully at a clay plug in the tapping hole. Taffy-sticky strands of orange metal drip to the sand, and suddenly a torrent of molten iron rushes out of the tapping hole, down the runner, and out into the sand channel with a sizzle and great fireworks sparks. The running stream rushes along the gates, seems to stop a moment as it fills up each pig, and then runs on to the next, the next, and the next. The molders prod the stream along with their skimmers, pulling bits of slag and sand eroded by the fiery stream. "Hey, lad"—Tom's calling you—"grab that skimmer next to you there and break out that little dam of sand keeping the pig from filling up. There you go."

The evening pour is finished. The ironmaster and his helper replace the broken-out clay plug with another. His skimmer rings against the stones and echoes around the arch as he cleans bits of iron off the runner stone and damstone. The iron pigs glow a deep, dusty red. The crew cleans up, waiting for the iron to cool and the next crew to arrive. Then they'll break the pigs off the gate metal with sledge hammers and load them on carts.

"Give us a hand, lad," Tom calls out. "We've got to get these pigs from the morning pour into the cart." It looks easy enough, a little pig of iron about four inches square and two feet long. Grunt! Why won't it come up out of the sand? Grunt! Darn, still won't move. Hey, how come Tom and the ironmaster and all the molders are falling down laughing? What's so funny, you guys?

"What's the matter, lad? That little pig's only a hundred pounds!" It looks as if you may not be cut out for ironmaking.

"Well, boy," the ironmaster says, still laughing and coming over to give you a hand, "you've been a big help today, mighty big help. How about staying on through the year? Tom here'll make a good molder out of you in no time." 53

Iron fences come in all manner of shapes and sizes and can be found in every town in America. This cast-iron masterpiece isn't in a museum, it's just down the street, at the Robert P. Dodge House in Georgetown, Washington, D.C.

Found Iron

9

A hundred years ago just about anything you could think of was made of iron. Iron was as much a part of people's lives then as steel, aluminum, alloys, and all kinds of plastics are part of ours. There were other metals in use—brass, tin, copper, zinc, bronze, even a little steel—but iron was the most useful and hardest working of them all.

At home, in those days, food was cooked in iron pots and skillets, stirred

The iron maker's craft showed even in simple, useful articles like this cast-iron coal chute cover in a sidewalk in Georgetown, Washington, D.C. Coal wagon drivers dumped coal down these chutes to the furnaces in the basements of houses and apartment buildings.

with iron spoons, on an iron stove. The frame of the bed was iron and so was the frame of the piano in the living room. There were iron runners on your sled, iron blades on your ice skates. Toy fire engines and locomotives were, just like the real ones, made of iron. Your parents would put on eyeglasses in delicate iron frames to work at an iron sewing machine or with iron carpenter's tools. Down in the basement of your apartment building, water heated in iron boilers flowed up iron pipes to bathtubs, kitchen sinks, and radiators all of iron. Other iron pipes in the walls brought illuminating gas to the lamps. Polly parrot sits in her cage of iron wire. Your front steps might be iron and, of course, the railings.

Once you're down those iron stairs, a list of iron things would become long if not impossible. Wooden street cars with iron fittings and wheels clattered and clanged down iron rails in the street dotted here and there with iron grates and manhold covers. Whole sidewalks might be iron. A short walk led past iron lamp posts, bridges, traffic lights, horse watering troughs, drinking fountains, hitching posts, and iron benches in the park. Doors swung on iron hinges and locked with iron keys. Wooden carriages and wagons on iron-rimmed wheels were pulled by horses shod with iron shoes. Your shoes clicked along the sidewalk and lasted longer with iron toe and heel plates. A policeman called his precinct from an iron call box (and wore a bright iron star). Machine tools, nails, the frames of your school desk, flag poles, nuts and bolts, thimbles, dentist chairs, and wheelchairs were all of iron. Windmills and axeheads, steamships, battleships and canal boats, printing presses, reapers, steam engines, plows, mailboxes, weathervanes and window frames, fences and wrenches. . . .

So where did it all go? Well, sometime in the late 1800s steel began to replace iron. Steel had been known of for centuries. Blacksmiths made small batches of steel in their forges. But it could only be made in small batches for very special uses, like knives, tools, and watch springs, so it was very expensive. Then new methods of converting iron to steel in large batches appeared, and steel became as available and inexpensive as iron. Iron rails were taken up and replaced with heavier, longer-lasting rails of steel. Engineers added steel parts to locomotives over the years until the ironhorse became a steelhorse. Buildings grew taller and became skyscrapers on frames of steel girders.

As common as iron was then, you'll have to look for it today. Surprisingly, much of it remains out on the streets, and American cities and farms are still open-air museums of ironmaking for you to explore.

Locomotives in the Park 10

You probably don't know any steam locomotives. Oh, they're around all right, a few standing quietly in parks and museums or out on an old, abandoned track somewhere. But to really *know* a steam locomotive is to be up close to one as it thunders by. It's as if you've been overtaken by an immense steel-gray giant. The ground trembles, a rush of wind tugs at your clothes and sucks your breath away. Silvery rods driving seven-foot-high spoked wheels dazzle the eye. Your ears fill with the roar and your face tingles with the heat of the firebox, where a mountain of coal burns to orange-red heat. Amid puffs of cindery smoke and hissing steam, rods and cranks and levers spin and slide back and forth like the works of some enormous clock. And from all this sound and movement comes a feeling of fearsome power, more power than you've ever been that close to.

Steam locomotives are some of the largest, most powerful machines ever built. Yet they were everywhere to be seen. While other steam engines worked hidden away in factory basements or below the waterline in huge ships, railroad locomotives were out and around. You could stand right next to one, even touch it (when you finally got up the courage), on a station platform or right at Main Street and Railroad Avenue, where dozens might come by in a single day. Steam locomotives were gentle giants. Men rode them like grand mythical horses, feeding their fires, urging them on from an inch-by-inch crawl to furious speeds, with but a touch of a gloved hand. They were named. Some were painted in splendid colors. Their bronze bells and whistles were kept polished bright. And to hear engineers talk about "their" locomotives you would have thought they were talking, not about machines, but about much respected old friends.

And then, suddenly, they were gone. In the 1940s a few diesel engines began to appear among tens of thousands of steam locomotives. The very last steam engine to be built in America came out of the shops in 1953. By 1954 only one out of every five trains was pulled by a steam locomotive. The life and

splendor of the wondrous gray giants ended quickly. By the early 1960s they were gone. After doing America's heaviest tasks for well over a century, the steam locomotive disappeared from the scene in a little over ten years!

Happily, not all of them ended up on a scrap heap. The railroads donated some to museums. Some they gave to towns along their route to be displayed in parks. Others continued to run during the summer months on "tourist" lines. Many were collected by ordinary people who loved old engines and wanted to have one around. And lots, it turns out, were just abandoned, left on a siding or out in the woods.

Wherever they've been hiding, old locomotives, long forgotten and unnoticed, are being "discovered," sometimes right in the middle of a large city. All kinds of people, from retired locomotive engineers and boilermakers to kids, are at work together, lovingly cleaning up abandoned little engines, fixing broken parts, scraping off years of rust, and putting on fresh coats of paint, rekindling their fires. And then they run them on old, rusty rails.

Chances are, you're not far from a railroad museum or tourist line where a reborn locomotive picks up passengers at a station built back in your great-great-grandparents' day. Of course, it's not exactly like the old days. Trains were a real part of American life then. Today, steam locomotives are artifacts, machines left over from a time long ago. But the magic is still there. The old puffing engine, the rhythm of the wheels and rail joints, and the smell of coal smoke take you back over the years in a way few other things can. That's because railroads grew up with this country, and the story of the steam locomotive is in many ways the story of America.

Steam locomotives, like most things we know of, didn't start out big. The first locomotives were quite small, so small that one builder called his *Tom Thumb*. But as small as *Tom Thumb* was, it turned out to be one of the most important inventions in America's history. *Tom Thumb* wasn't the first locomotive in America. The first locomotives, like so many of our ideas and customs, came from England. One of the earliest of these was the *Stourbridge Lion*. Another, *John Bull*, was built by the English inventor Robert Stephenson, known and respected in America for his designs. But *Tom Thumb* will always be remembered as the first locomotive built here in America to pull a train of passengers.

Tom Thumb was the idea of a New York merchant, Peter Cooper. Peter,

Members of the Pacific Locomotive Association work weekends, lovingly restoring old locomotives and running them on their own railroad, the Castro Point Railway Museum in Richmond, California. All over the country now, on weekends and during the summer, little railroads are coming alive again with the sounds and smells of steam power.

born in 1791, had very little schooling, but he did have a lot of experience from many interesting jobs. As a young man Peter had worked as a carriage maker, a cloth cutter, a machinist, a salesman, and a grocer. Later, Peter and some friends started an iron works, and it was here that his idea for a little engine took shape. At that time, and for many years afterward, locomotives were made of iron and wood. Along the way Peter had picked up just the skills he needed— carriage building and metalworking. Now he had a shop to make the heavy iron parts a steam locomotive would need. So the work began and for two years Peter and his crew worked on their locomotive. They had few formulas to work with; not much was known about the properties of metals in those days. Peter would work out the shape of a part, make one, and try it out. If it failed he would make it stronger or change its shape, each time trying it out until it worked. He had studied the designs of earlier locomotives and used their most successful ideas. Finally, in the summer of 1830, *Tom Thumb* stood at the Canton Iron Works in Baltimore, Maryland, ready to run. Peter would now have to call on another of the skills learned in his youth. He would try to sell the directors of the Baltimore & Ohio Railroad his idea of a steam locomotive.

Baltimore. August 28, 1830. The day for *Tom Thumb*'s trial run had arrived. Behind the little engine was an open car filled with Baltimore & Ohio Railroad directors and a few of Peter's friends. The run would be to Ellicott's Mills, about thirteen miles away, and back. Peter was the engineer. He set the fire under the boiler, taking pieces of cordwood from the stack at his feet. Water for the boiler came from a small wooden barrel. Everyone watched Peter work. Soon there came the hiss of steam getting louder and louder as the pressure in the boiler went higher, and suddenly *Tom Thumb* with its boat-shaped car of startled passengers lurched off down the track.

The trainload of shouting, excited passengers made the trip to the Mills in less than an hour. But if the trip up was thrilling, wait until you hear about what happened on the way back. *Tom Thumb* got into a race . . . well, let's hear the story from one of Peter's friends who was there that day:

> The great stagecoach company of the day was Stockton & Stokes; and on this occasion a gallant gray of great beauty and power was attached to another car on the second track, and met the engine at the Relay House on the way back. From this point it was decided to have a race home; and the

start being even, away went horse and engine, the snort of the one and the puff of the other keeping time and tune. At first the gray had the best of it. The horse was perhaps a quarter of a mile ahead when the safety valve of the engine lifted. The blower whistled, the steam blew off in vapory clouds, the pace increased, the passengers shouted, the engine gained on the horse, soon it lapped him—the whip was applied, the race was neck and neck, nose and nose—then the engine passed the horse, and a great hurrah hailed the victory.

But *Tom Thumb* didn't make it to the finish line. Just as the gray's master was about to give up, something on the engine snapped. A drive belt to the blower had broken. Peter, who was working feverishly as both engineer and fireman, tried to get the belt back on its pulley. No use. *Tom Thumb* came to a rolling, wheezing stop. Peter Cooper had lost the race that day but not his argument. The steam engine, not the horse, would power American railroads in the years to come.

Not even Peter Cooper could have imagined how the steam locomotive would grow. It happened not over the years but within months. *Tom Thumb* weighed about 1800 pounds, less than a ton, lighter and shorter than a small automobile. In November—not three months after the race—*The Best Friend of Charleston* began running on the South Carolina Railroad, weighing 10,000 pounds. *Best Friend* could pull five cars holding about fifty passengers at over

twenty miles per hour. Every year after that, heavier locomotives that could pull longer trains of passenger and freight cars would be built, from 11,000 pounds in the 1830s

to 115,000 pounds in the 1860s

to 190,000 pounds in the 1890s,

to 500,000 pounds in the 1920s,

and in the 1940s—little more than a century after *Tom Thumb*'s race with the gray—came *Big Boy*, with sixteen big drive wheels and the power to pull trains of hundreds of freight cars,

weighing over a million pounds! So immense was *Big Boy*'s firebox—235 inches long by 96 inches wide—that *Tom Thumb* and the whole car of cheering, wildly waving Baltimore & Ohio directors might have fit inside.

Between *Tom Thumb* and *Big Boy* locomotives changed in a lot of important ways. More drive wheels were added—six, eight, ten, twelve, sixteen—for greater traction, pulling power.

Wondering how old a found locomotive is? Would you like to know where it was built? The answers to these questions and the name of the builder can be found on the builder's plate, usually on the right-hand side of the smokebox, under the stack. Builder's plates on locomotives from the late 1800s were often mounted up front, right in the middle of the smokebox cover.

Lead trucks of two, four, and, eventually, six wheels were added up front to support longer locomotives and guide them into and around curves. Behind the drivers trailing trucks of two, four, and six wheels were added to support bigger fireboxes. The first locomotives of *Tom Thumb*'s day burned wood in their fireboxes to heat water to steam. Later, in the 1860s and 1870s, coal replaced wood. By 1900 many locomotives burned oil. Locomotive builders had different ways of doing this or that on an engine. Each might have a different-looking cab or firebox design, something special about the smokestack or some difference in shape. And in the 1930s and 1940s some steam locomotives were streamlined. But down deep inside, in the firebox and the boiler, the *basic* idea of steam power never changed. It may be hard for you to believe, looking at the two locomotives side by side, but *Big Boy* is just a large, very large *Tom Thumb*.

66   Some people laughed at Peter Cooper's locomotive, calling it "a teakettle

on wheels." But steam engines are easy to understand if we think of them as just that, giant teakettles. Peter began with the "teakettle," the boiler, made of sheet iron rolled into a curved shape and riveted together to make a cylinder. Inside was a tank to hold water and collect the steam. At the bottom of the boiler was a firebox for burning sticks of wood. And at the top was a smokestack, tall enough to carry smoke, sparks, and cinders over the engineer's head (which never seemed to work) and cause a draft through the firebox.

Tom Thumb's boiler was not a new invention. Steam engines had already been in use for years to power machinery, grind flour, spin yarn and weave cloth, grind up sugar cane, and do all kinds of work. These were called "sta-

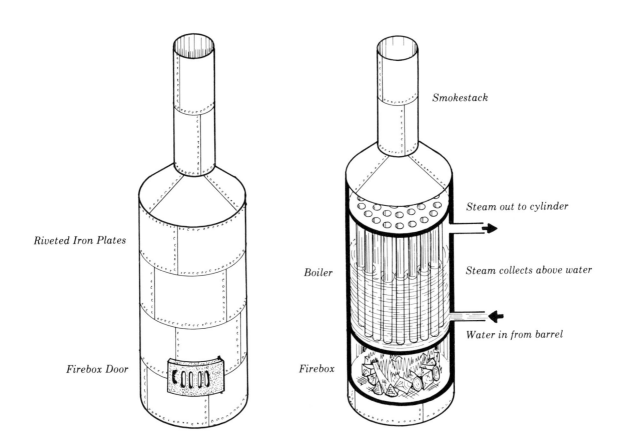

Smokestack

Riveted Iron Plates

Boiler

Steam out to cylinder

Steam collects above water

Water in from barrel

Firebox Door

Firebox

tionary engines" because they did their work standing still. Their boilers were big iron tanks of water heated by a fire underneath until the water boiled and turned into steam. Because only the water at the bottom of the boiler was heated directly by the flame, it took a long time to get up enough steam, much too long to run a locomotive. Besides, steam locomotives needed more steam, a lot more steam than most stationary engines. This was Peter's problem, and to solve it he would have to redesign the teakettle.

Peter found a better way in some plans for a boiler drawn by Nathan Read back in 1790. Read never actually built a boiler from his plans, but his idea was to run a bunch of tubes from the firebox up through the boiler to the smokestack. Read figured that the fire would heat the water at the bottom of the boiler and then travel up through the tubes and heat the rest of the water, too. All this doesn't seem very important if you're just heating a few cups of water for tea. But what if you had to heat hundreds or thousands of gallons of water to boiling to get the steam you need to run a locomotive for hours and hours? To Peter, Nathan Read's idea made a lot of sense. He would try it out.

So, through *Tom Thumb*'s boiler Peter ran iron tubes—musket barrels, actually—between the firebox and the smokestack. It worked. When he got the fire going, the water came to a boil quickly, and soon lots of steam collected in the space above the water. And that's exactly how it works in any steam locomotive, even *Big Boy*. You could easily climb through *Big Boy*'s firebox doors, and once inside (where there's room as well for twenty or thirty of your friends) you'd face a huge steel wall with hundreds of round holes. These are one end of the long tubes running from the firebox, through the enormous boiler (almost nine feet in diameter by fifty feet long!) to the smokebox up front.

Once Peter had enough steam it was a simple matter to put it to work. This would be done with a cylinder that was not very different from the cylinders on stationary engines of the day. Inside the cylinder is a flat, round disk or piston attached to a rod going through one end of the cylinder, the piston rod. The piston rod was attached to a drive rod that went to a crank on one pair of *Tom Thumb*'s wheels.

And that's how it all began. To make steam engines more powerful, more steam was needed. To get more steam, fireboxes and boilers got bigger and bigger. And, of course, larger and larger cylinders would be needed and more of them. *Tom Thumb*'s little upright boiler was enlarged in later locomotives

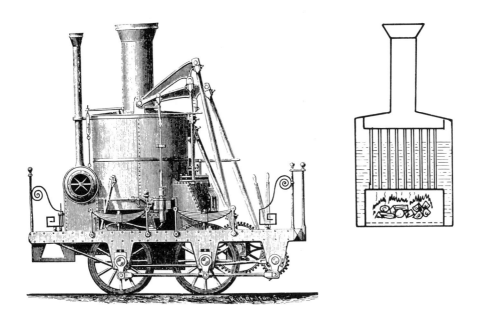

until, unable to get any taller, it was "bent" in the middle. The firebox was still upright but now the boiler was horizontal.

And over the years fireboxes, boilers, and locomotives grew longer

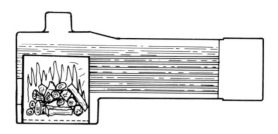

and longer,

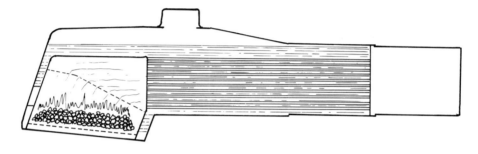

and longer,

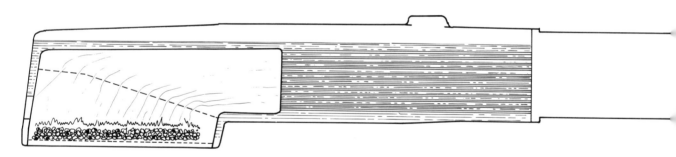

as fireboxes and boilers became bigger. Looking back now, it's hard to believe how the steam locomotive has grown. *Tom Thumb*'s cylinder was 3¼ inches in diameter and 14 inches long. *Big Boy* had four cylinders, the largest 26 inches by 32 inches. During *Tom Thumb*'s two-hour trip to the Mills and back Peter had to work hard keeping a few sticks of cordwood in the firebox. In that same amount of time *Big Boy* would burn 50,000 pounds of coal!

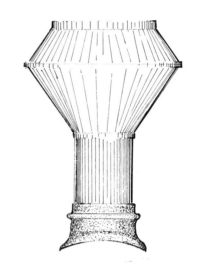

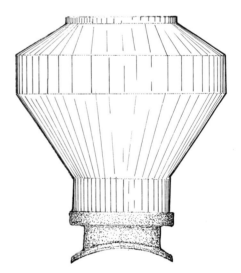

Smokestacks are an easy-to-spot clue to the kind of fuel a locomotive burned in its firebox, wood or coal. Both of the stacks on the right, the diamond (top) and balloon stack (bottom), are the mark of a wood-burning locomotive. Inside were baffles and screen to keep sparks from setting fire to the countryside. On the left are an earlier (late 1800s to early 1900s) and more modern stack found on coal-burning locomotives. There's no difference between the stacks on coal- and oil-burning locomotives.

Locomotives have names, too. Some are descriptive names, like Mastodon and Centipede. Some, like the Santa Fe and Union Pacific, are named for the railroad that designed and ordered the first of its type from a locomotive builder. And others are, well, just names that have become tradition down through the years. American was one of the first locomotives built in this country at a time when many were imported from England. Railroad historians and engineers refer to locomotives by a series of numbers that show the arrangement of the wheels. For instance, a Pacific is also called a 4-6-2 because it has four small wheels in the lead truck (two on each side),

◁ ○ ○

six large driving wheels (three on each side),

◁ ○ ○ ◯ ◯ ◯

and two small wheels in the trailing truck.

◁ ○ ○ ◯ ◯ ◯ ○

Big Boy had two sets of driving wheels, sixteen in all! So it's called a 4-8-8-4, with a four-wheel leading truck up front,

◁ ○ ○

a set of eight drivers,

◁ ○ ○ ◯ ◯ ◯ ◯

a second set of eight drivers,

◁ ○ ○ ◯ ◯ ◯ ◯ ◯ ◯

and four small wheels in the trailing truck.

◁ ○ ○ ◯ ◯ ◯ ◯ ◯ ◯ ○ ○

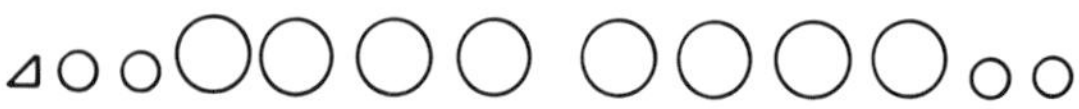

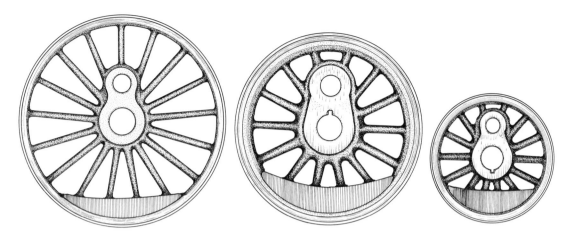

Left to right: *High-stepping, graceful drivers for fast passenger locomotives; low, powerful drivers (50″ to 68″) used on massive freight locomotives; little drivers (36″ to 52″) got nimble logging locomotives and switch engines around tight turns*

Drive Wheels Big and Small

Some locomotives you'll find will have big drive wheels, standing high above your head. Yet others will have wheels so small you can easily rest your hand on top of them. How come? Well, locomotives did different kinds of work and needed drive wheels of different diameters. Here's a guide to help you tell what kind of work a locomotive did from the size of the drive wheels.

Passenger locomotives, for instance, were built for speed. Back in the 1890s railroads competed with one another to see who had the fastest passenger trains. One locomotive, the New York Central's No. 999, reached 112.5 miles per hour, pulling a train between Batavia and Buffalo, New York. To go that fast it needed huge driving wheels, over seven feet tall!

Freight locomotives, however, have to pull long trains of over a hundred heavily loaded cars up over mountain ranges. They were larger, heavier, and had more—eight, ten, twelve, sixteen, even twenty-four—drivers, which were smaller to give the locomotive more pulling power.

Switch engines, logging locomotives, and small locomotives used inside factories had to have small wheels to move easily around tight curves.

Atlantic Locomotive

1 Headlight
2 Number plate
3 Smokebox door
4 Smoke stack
5 Smokebox
6 Front boiler brace
7 Front bumper step
8 Flag staff
9 Coupler
10 Pilot
11 Front bumper

12 Lead or pilot truck
13 Piston
14 Piston rod
15 Front cylinder head
16 Cross head
17 Air tank
18 Running boards
19 Hand rail
20 Headlight step
21 Builder's plate
22 Bell

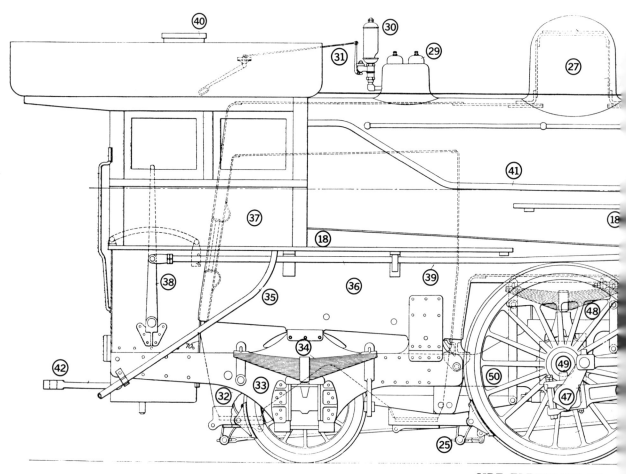

SIDE ELEVATION OF

PLATE III.

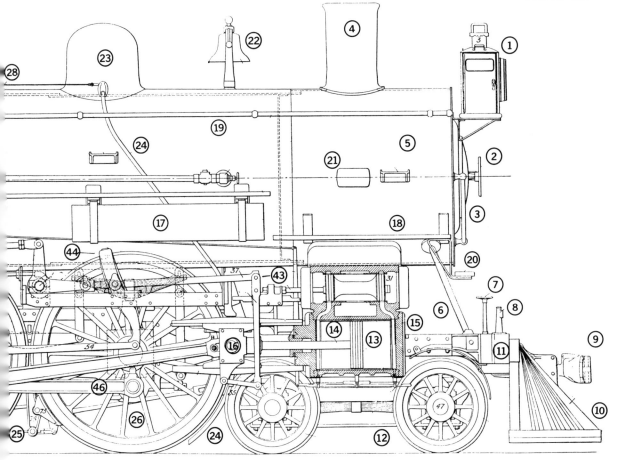

ATLANTIC LOCOMOTIVE.

Covered bridges are among the oldest in America and are the hiding places of some of the earliest wooden trusses. This one, near Covington, Virginia, was built in 1835.

Bridges

11

As a novice historian you may be noticing for the first time how entwined events seem to be, how one event seems always to lead to another. Some of that has to do with how you choose the events and arrange them, but it really does happen that way lots of times. Historians call this "cause and effect," and it shows up clearly when people start building things.

Take railroad locomotives, bridges, and iron, for example. For centuries the heaviest load a bridge builder could imagine was a wagon or two pulled by oxen, maybe twenty tons. Wooden bridges worked fine over streams and small rivers. Wide and wild rivers were difficult to span and so became barriers to business and travel. If you had to cross a wide river there were ferries at the busiest crossings, or the road just went down to the water's edge at the best fording spot and continued up the bank on the other side.

Then, in a few years, the locomotive changed that. Just fifty years or so after *Stourbridge Lion* (seven tons) and *Tom Thumb* (less than a ton), iron spans hundreds of feet long carried locomotives weighing hundreds of thousands of pounds. What's more, thousands of bridges had been built over thousands of creeks, gullies, ravines, gorges, rivers, canyons, roads, and tracks. A few decades later, when two *Big Boys* double-heading a hundred-car freight train rolled onto a steel bridge, the load was more than two million pounds!

A hundred years, that's all. It seems a long time to you, but all that occurred within two generations, three at the most (and included your grandparents). An apprentice carpenter starting out building timber trusses would live to see them replaced by trusses of iron. His son would learn to build trusses he hadn't heard of with girders of new high-strength steels. Fortunately, the history of these bridge builders did not happen so long ago that it's been lost. Of the thousands and thousands of bridges built over those years, many remain, a few of each type, to tell the story of bridge building in America. One or two of them are not very far away.

The first big railroad bridges used a centuries-old idea. Long and high bridges were made of stone. Masonry bridges are impressive, beautiful structures; they're strong and last forever. The Thomas Viaduct near Relay, Maryland, is 600 feet long. When it was built in the early 1830s, little engines puffed across it like toys. Over the years, though, it has carried some of the heaviest locomotives built and still, today, carries long, heavy freight trains. The Starrucca Viaduct is another beautiful example of early American stonework and still works today, 140 years after it was built.

The stone masons who built these graceful hundred-foot high arches to carry the Erie Railway across Starrucca Creek Valley, in Susquehanna County, Pennsylvania, back in 1847 could not have imagined the length and weight of the trains crossing them today. This kind of stonework is called rock-faced coursed ashlar, because the masons left a rough surface on the face we can see and laid them in even courses.

But bridges of stone could not be the answer for long. For one thing, stone bridges are expensive. Large crews of stone cutters, carters, masons, and mortar mixers worked for years to quarry, shape, haul, and set thousands and thousands of stone blocks. Towering wooden scaffolds called "falsework" had to be built upward following the progress of the work and supporting the arches until they were finished. There was always the danger of a sudden storm and downpour turning the dry riverbed into a raging torrent of angry water in minutes, carrying away falsework and workers. And in many parts of the country there just isn't enough of the right kind of stone. But the real problem was time. Bridge crews working in stone could not possibly keep up with track crews. Between 1880 and 1890 130,000 miles of track were laid! Along any one track a dozen bridges might be needed in a single day.

The choice of railroad builders was the truss bridge. The trusses, or sides of the bridge, were at first made of wood. Wood was available everywhere along the right of way. Trees could be cut down and hewn into bridge members right on the spot. Trusses were easily built up of small sticks that could be hauled by wagon or on a railroad flatcar. And they went up fast. Once the wooden members had been cut to size and drilled, a bridge crew could easily assemble a truss bridge in a few days, sometimes in a single twelve-hour working day.

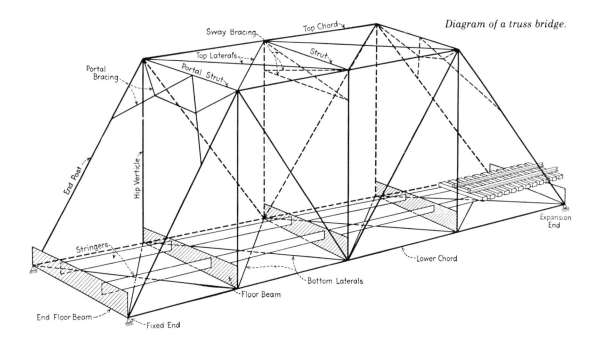

Diagram of a truss bridge.

Truss bridges can be made to support a lot of weight even though the individual parts seem small. The two trusses that make the sides of the bridge hold up the deck on which the road or track is laid. The principle is actually simple, and you can make a simple cardboard model of a truss bridge that shows you exactly how it works. First, span a couple of books with a piece of cardboard about twelve inches long by five or six inches wide. Then place a weight in the middle.

Sag. Not much support there. But that's what would happen if you tried to support a train with a flat deck. Now, scribe a line down both sides of your bridge with a ballpoint pen, about an inch from each edge. Fold the two sections up along the lines, place the bridge across the books, and replace the weight.

The folded sides become trusses stiffening and supporting the deck of your bridge. By the way, if you round off each corner and draw some lines down the sides you'll have a model of the plate girder bridges you'll see where railroad tracks cross over streets and roads.

You've built what engineers call a "pony" or "half-through" truss. If you turn your model over so that the deck's on top and the bridge rests on the ends of the trusses, it becomes a "deck" truss.

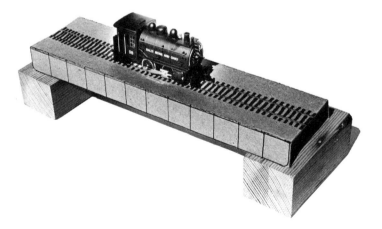

Bridge engineers discovered another relationship very early. See what happens when you glue two new trusses on your bridge, the same length but about six inches high (or you might fold a new bridge with deeper trusses).

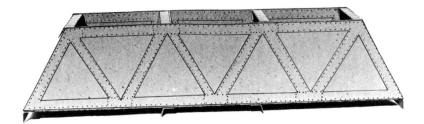

The deeper truss is able to support more. But then there's the troublesome buckling, and if you study your model carefully you'll see exactly what's causing it. As the floor begins to sag it pulls the trusses in at the top and the bridge fails. The very first thing you learned was that trusses must stand upright to support the load; they have no strength lying flat. It's probably already occurred to you what needs to be done. That's just what a bridge builder would do. . . .

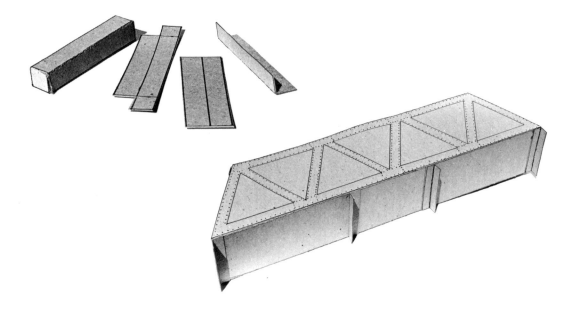

A few folded cardboard floor beams glued under the deck keep it from sagging and pulling the trusses out of alignment . . .

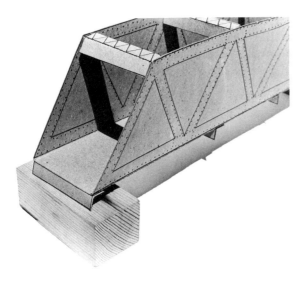

and a few cardboard struts glued between the two trusses at the top help them resist buckling (and vibrating in a strong crosswind). This last step—deepening the trusses and adding struts across the top—turned your model into a "through" truss bridge. If you turned this bridge upside down it, too, would work as a deck truss that's deeper, stiffer, and stronger than your first model. Of course, it needs more clearance under the track or roadway and couldn't be used over a small creek. But that's one of the considerations when a bridge builder is deciding whether to use a deck or through truss.

Making models is more than just playing. It's fun, for sure, but it's also the only way to *feel* how a bridge works. You could *know* how a truss works by reading about it. But America's first bridge builders, like you, really understood bridges by building them. You've built a complete truss bridge and understand how each of the parts—trusses, struts, floor beams—work. You've actually observed a truss and a deck fail and know now how to correct each problem. You've discovered why folding a piece of metal once or twice along its length, turning it into an angle or channel, makes it more useful than a flat bar. And you've learned a lot about the history of bridges. If you decide to build a model two, three, six feet long or a real bridge you've learned how to go about it.

Early American bridge builders experimented with models of their bridges, too. They built their models of small wooden sticks scaled down from the real bridge. For example, they might decide to build a model 1/100th the size of the real bridge. If the planned bridge was to be 100 feet long, the model would be 1 foot long. Then each piece would be made to this scale, exactly 1/100th the size of the bridge to be built. A bridge 1/100th the size of a real bridge, the builder would reason, should be able to support 1/100th of the load. So the bridge model was loaded with small weights. If a member broke, it was replaced with a larger one. Weights were added again. The builder looked for sagging and buckling, then added members to support the deck or stiffen the trusses. Eventually, the model was holding two or three times the load it was expected to hold. This was the builder's safety factor. And it's why many old bridges eventually carried loads many times what they were designed to carry.

You'll get to know some of these early craftsmen who built America's first truss bridges when you begin to recognize their work. It's not likely you'll find one of their original bridges, one built back in the 1830s or 1840s (then, again, who knows?), but their original designs and their names have lasted over the years. Engineers still refer to a truss as a Warren, a Fink, a Howe, a Waddell, a Bollman, a Post, or as the work of one of many other builders. So even if you find a fairly modern bridge of steel, its truss form is a direct descendant of the first ones made of wood well over a century ago. Pretty soon you'll be spotting them easily.

Recognizing truss forms takes a little practice, that's all. It's a little confusing at first. Your first reaction, like that of most people just beginning to look at bridges, will probably be that they look so much alike. They're all just a maze of triangles!

Well, that in itself is an important observation. Trusses are all combinations of triangles, and there's good reason for that. Let's make another model to find out about triangles, this time using some strips of cardboard one inch by about six inches and one about nine inches long. Start by making a square with four strips held together at the corner with paper fasteners. Then make a triangle with three more pieces.

84

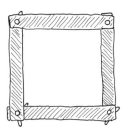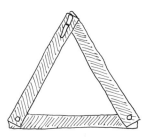

Stand the square up and push against one side and watch what hap . . .

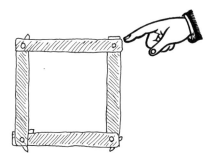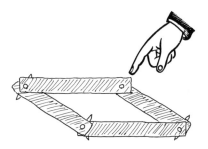

Oops, it collapsed. Now push against one side of your triangle. Go ahead, push harder. Quite a difference. Three-sided figures can't be distorted as easily as four-sided figures, which is why the triangle is the basic element in just about every kind of truss. Can you figure a way to strengthen that square so it won't collapse so easily? Right. Just put in a diagonal brace and make two triangles.

Sometime back in the Middle Ages an unknown builder discovered the triangle's strength and used it to support heavy roofs by adding a king post in the center. Later, someone discovered that king post trusses could be used to support a wooden deck and make a bridge.

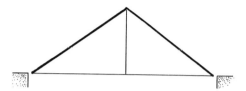

You can trace with your finger (or work out on a cardboard model) the movement of forces through a king post truss. Imagine a heavy weight in the middle of the bridge. The weight pulls down on the king post. And the king post pulls down on the two timbers sloping downward toward the ends of the bridge, carrying the force out to the bridge supports. King post trusses are for little bridges up to about sixty feet. But if you understand how they work, you can understand spans hundreds of feet long.

Architect Ithiel Town, one of America's first bridge builders, figured that if the triangle is so strong, lots of triangles would be even stronger. He began building lattice trusses in the 1820s,

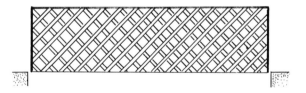

scores of triangles overlapping. His first bridges were made of hundreds of sticks of wood about two inches thick and ten inches wide. Everything was fastened together with wooden pins called "treenails." (Iron nails were hard to get and expensive in those days.) Later lattice trusses of iron straps were built for

86

railroad bridges. Some wooden Town lattice trusses have lasted a long, long time, and you can still find them hidden inside covered bridges.

Thomas and Caleb Pratt must have been playing with squares and triangles, because they strengthened the rectangles in their truss with a single diagonal brace just as you did.

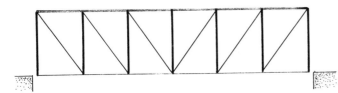

William Howe's trusses had two diagonals of heavy timbers in each rectangle, or panel, making them stiffer and sturdier than Pratt trusses. They were the most often used wooden truss on the railroads in the 1800s, and they show up in a lot of old photographs from those days.

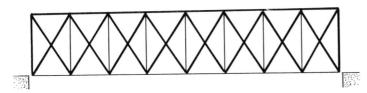

James Warren discovered he could build bridges up to 400 feet long with triangles lined end to end,

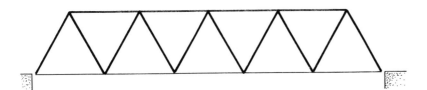

87

Squire Whipple ran diagonals across two panels,

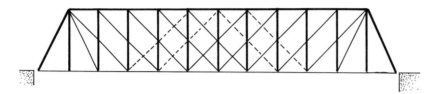

Albert Fink put king posts inside king posts inside king posts,

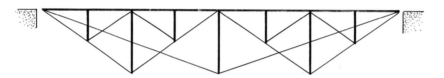

and Stephen Long turned triangles up on end to make a K-truss. Long's first K-trusses, built in the 1840s, were made of wood. A century later modern engineers built steel K-truss bridges over 600 feet long!

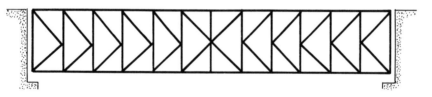

These are but a few of the many trusses that appeared during the 1800s. A couple—Warren and Pratt—have been the favorites of engineers all these years and are still being built. They're everywhere, and you'll learn to recognize them first. Then, just a little farther on, you'll spot a Parker, Camelback, Baltimore, or Pennsylvania. But the real fun comes with finding a bridge that doesn't seem to be any of these. There's something about it. That pretty bit of ornamental ironwork. And those long, thin rods floating through the air. It's old, all right. Is it a Whipple? There were once a lot of them around. Maybe it's one of the hundreds of Wendel Bollman's trusses the railroads built a century ago. Couldn't be. Why, only one of those has been found in all these years and . . . say, maybe you'd better check the Bridgefinder's Alphabet (pages 91-95).

deck truss

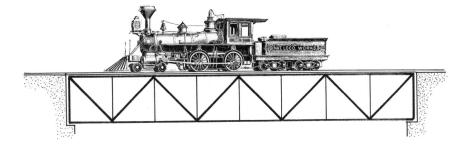

half-through (pony) truss

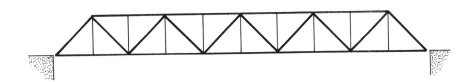

through truss

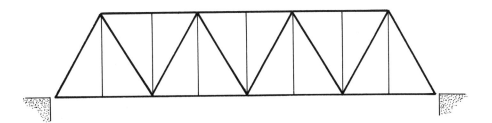

A bridge. Should be pretty easy to find, right? Thirty feet high. Couple hundred feet long. Tons and tons of iron or steel. Painted bright green or silver or orange. Couldn't miss it.

Someday you might be walking down an old road (good place to look for old bridges) and come upon something like this.

Not very impressive. If you're like most of the thousands of people who have walked or driven over this spot you'll just go on. But you're a historian, an industrial archaeologist. There's always more to something than meets the eye. So you walk back a few yards, climb down a grassy embankment a ways, and. . .

Eye bar

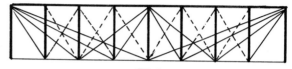

Fink

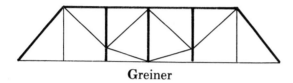

Greiner

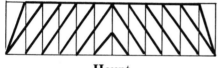

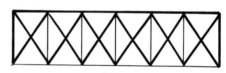

Haupt

Howe

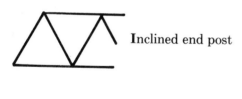

Inclined end post

Joint

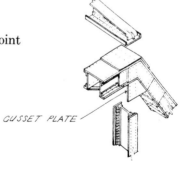

GUSSET PLATE

PIN

EYE BARS
(DIAGONALS)

WOW, look at that! Wonder what it is. Let's see if it's in the Bridgefinder's Alphabet here. Hmmm . . . lots of rods going every which way. Can't be a Fink or a Bollman or a Kellogg, because the rods run parallel to each other. Each rod crosses two panels . . . so it's got to be a . . . Whipple, double intersection truss. Right. It's all cast and wrought iron. (Old timers hereabouts know it was built in the 1880s. It happens to be the oldest iron bridge still in service on a road anywhere in California.) It's not really one of Squire Whipple's original bridges. Dozens of companies were making Whipple-like bridges then, including the Phoenix Iron Co., whose name is all over this one. It was, in those days, a favorite of highway and railroad bridge engineers. Sit down there in the shade, rest a minute, and look at some real nineteenth-century American bridge engineering. Now, aren't you glad you stopped?

Bridgefinder's Alphabet

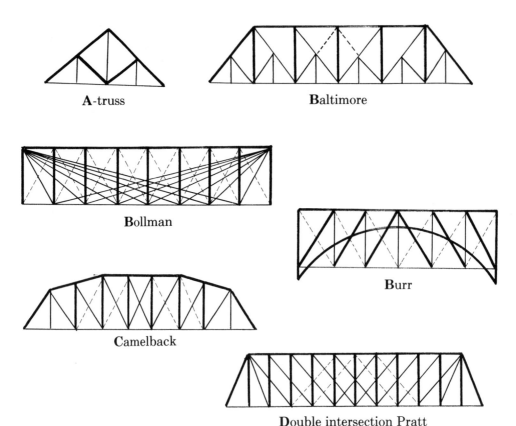

A-truss

Baltimore

Bollman

Burr

Camelback

Double intersection Pratt

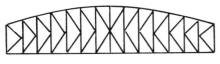

K-truss

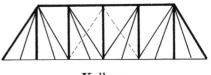

Kellogg

Lane

Lenticular

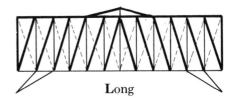

Long

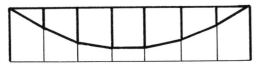

McGuffie

Name plate

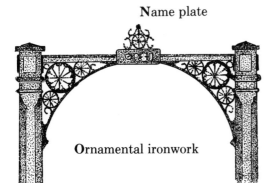

Ornamental ironwork

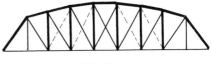

Parker

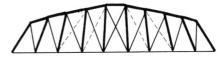

Pegram

Pennsylvania

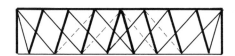

Post

Pratt

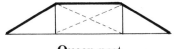

Queen post

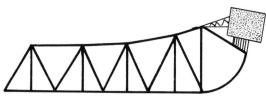

Rolling lift

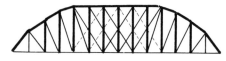

Schwedler

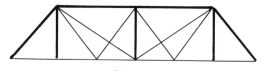

Stearns

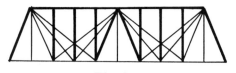

Thacher

94

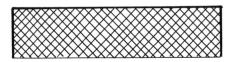

Town lattice

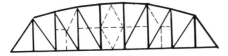

Unrecognizable bridges are often old
ones strengthened with a few extra
ties and struts like this Parker

Vierendeel

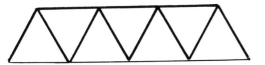

Warren

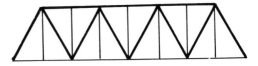

Whipple's bowstring arch-truss

X is for an unknown bridge
you might discover

Your found bridge sketch

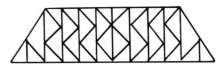

Z-truss

The largest railroad viaduct in the United States stretches 2,053 feet across the Kinzua Creek Valley in McKean County, Pennsylvania. The first viaduct here was built in 1882 and was replaced with the present one of steel in 1900, 301 feet high.

Viaducts and Trestles 12

These are two special kinds of bridges. Viaducts carry roads, railroads, and walkways over land, and are often found spanning wide valleys. Earlier viaducts, like the Thomas and Starrucca, were made of stone, and later ones, like the Kinzua Viaduct, were made of metal. However they were made, viaducts are some of the most spectacular structures you'll find. The Kinzua Viaduct is over 2000 feet long and rises 300 feet high above the valley floor.

You'll see a lot of railroad trestles if you travel or live out West. That's because railroad builders found the trestle well suited to the deep, V-shaped gorges and cuts they encountered. When wooden bridges were the only choice, railroad engineers preferred the trestle because it can support heavier loads and better withstand the high winds and stopping, swaying, and acceleration of heavy locomotives. Besides, the posts and timbers needed for trestles—iron bolts, nuts, and washers are the only "bought" parts in a trestle—could be taken from the forests all along the way. The trunks of the Sugar, Yellow, Jeffrey, and other pines that grow in the Sierras, some over 200 feet tall, were perfect for trestle posts.

Railroads run alongside and within easy view of a lot of highways and roads

Railroad trestles of heavy timbers are a common sight along highways throughout the western states, spanning little creeks, like this one, or deep river gorges.

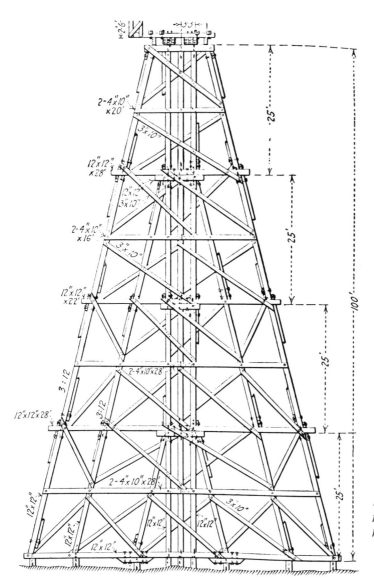

An engineer's drawing
for a trestle 100
feet high.

in the West. You can spot a trestle by its A-shaped bents all tied together by a spiderweb of braces. After these were put up, heavy timbers called stringers were run along the top from one bent to the next. And on top of the stringers were laid the ties and rails. Some wooden trestles built early in the last century were replaced by truss bridges. The Kinzua Viaduct is steel and replaced an earlier one like it of iron.

This is a trestle, too, a steel one. Many wooden trestles are still in use after more than a century. But as locomotives, trains, and traffic got heavier railroads replaced their timber trestles with iron and then steel trestles like this one. If you look closely you'll see that this is actually three bridges in one—a Warren deck truss (left), two trestle bents and plate girders running along the top.

A glance upward in an old building is often rewarded with a sight like this, a maze of wooden roof trusses. These support the roof over the huge Baltimore & Ohio rail rolling mill in Cumberland, Maryland, built in 1869.

Bridges in the Attic 13

Once you start thinking about trusses, learning their names, and looking for them, you'll begin seeing them everywhere, even up under the roof! Don't worry, you're not just seeing things. The roof trusses you'll find exposed in railroad stations, the gymnasium at school, any large, open building usually, are just like bridge trusses.

Roof trusses and bridge trusses work in exactly the same way. Some support the roof on their top chord (like deck trusses). Others support the roof or ceiling with their bottom chord. Roof trusses, too, have been made of wood, wood and iron, iron and steel over the years. You'll see truckloads of prefabricated wooden trusses being delivered to house sites today (and there are probably several hidden up in your attic right now). They have the same familiar forms and names—Warren, Fink, Howe, Pratt, and so on. They even had the same encouragement to grow—the railroads. Train sheds were needed to span dozens and dozens of tracks. As locomotives, the machinery to make them, and the spaces to assemble them got bigger and bigger, the roofs to cover them did, too. Factories, auditoriums, lots of different kinds of other buildings were also getting bigger.

So engineers began experimenting with all kinds of truss forms that would allow longer and longer clear spans without columns in the middle. And that's why you're seeing bridges in the attic.

Roof Trusses

Queen rod

King post, or king rod

Two-hinged arch

*Three-hinged steel arch
(for spans of 125 feet
and over)*

Howe, or English

Howe
*The diagonals are in
compression.*

Howe trussed arch

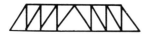

*Howe (top chord flat or
with slight slope)*

Howe (with counters)

Flat Pratt

*Pratt (steel or
combination of wood
and steel)*

Pratt
*The diagonals are in
tension.*

*Long-span subdivided
Pratt truss*

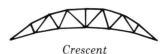

Crescent

Belgian
*The diagonals are
perpendicular to the top
chords.*

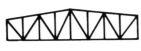

Warren

Warren with monitor

Flat Warren

Subdivided Warren

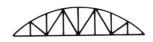

Bowstring

Cambered Fink

Fink, or compound Fink

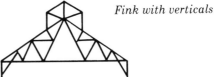

Fink with verticals

Fink
This is a variation of the
Fink truss shown in
the bridge diagram.

Compound Fink truss

Fink with monitor

Fan

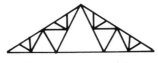

Fan, or compound fan

Fan Fink

Sawtooth
This truss is generally
used to allow natural
lighting of large floor
areas.

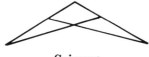

Scissors

Silvery rails and smooth brown paving bricks from another century remind us of the route of an old street railway. The slot in the center rails marks this as a cable railway. Under the street ran a long continuous cable to which the cars grabbed on and were pulled along.

Fares, Please

14

A glimmer of silvery rail, a few rough paving bricks showing through the broken pavement. That may be all that's left to see of a street railway in your neighborhood. Street railways were our first transit systems. For a small fare you could now travel around big cities or even out to small outlying towns. Cities took great pride in their street railways, painting the streetcars beautiful colors. Manufacturers' advertisements emphasized the quality and beauty of their cars, like this one for the Omnibus & Street Railway Car Business (1876):

> The firm employs about 300 skilled hands in the various departments, all of whom are practical men, many of whom are artists and special experts in their business. The painting and ornamentation of streetcars is a delicate matter, and can be performed only by skillful artists.

The earliest street railway cars were pulled by a team of horses. Later, steam cars appeared and were used into the early part of this century when streetcars were electrified. There were once hundreds of streetcar cities but, sadly, most of the brightly painted little cars, clattering and clanging their way down the center of the street, disappeared in the 1950s.

Baldwin steam motors pulling a streetcar went into service in Baltimore, Dubuque, Iowa, and several other cities in the late 1870s.

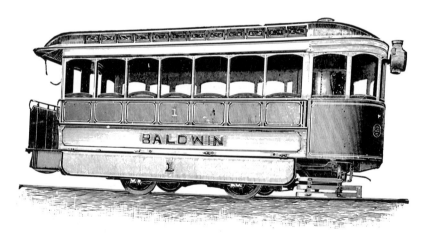

If you look through the front windows of this Baldwin steam streetcar, you can see the vertical boiler inside. Cars like this began running along streets in Philadelphia and Brooklyn in 1875.

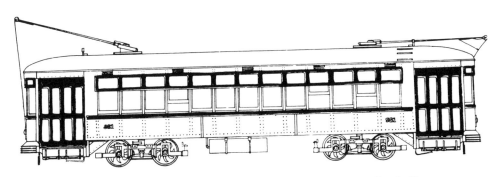

Streetcars like this one running today on the St. Charles Avenue line in New Orleans, Louisiana, were built back in 1923. Streetcars have operated on this line since 1835, making it the oldest continuously run street railway in the world.

Early horse-drawn street railway cars.

Electro Vapor Engine.

GAS OR GASOLINE FOR FUEL.

70612 No fire: no boiler: no engineer: no danger. You turn the switch, engine does the rest. Engine run by spark from small battery. The cost of running: In computing the cost of running, the following facts should be taken into consideration.

I. No expense until started.

II. No necessity of starting until the power is required.

III Expense while running always in exact proportion to amount of power used.

IV. The moment engine stops all expense stops. When running at maximum speed and power, our engine consumes about one-eighth gallon of gasoline per horse-power per hour, or, when illuminating gas is used, twenty cubic feet of gas per indicated horse-power per hour.

Inventions that change our lives in important ways usually go unnoticed at first. During one of your visits to the library you might come across a little advertisement like this one for the "Electro Vapor Engine." But you'll have to look carefully; it's way in the back of an 1895 catalog. So what? Well, "You turn the switch, engine does the rest," and . . . the steam engine has just become obsolete!

Rainy Day Explorations 15

Some day, when it's too dreary, cold, and wet to look for history outside, find a warm, comfortable library. It's probably not occurred to you, but there is a lot of old engineering there: bridges, locomotives, canal boats, waterwheels, and lots more. What's more, you can watch a locomotive being built, a canal being dug, or look in on a factory of a century ago. You'll experience the excitement people felt when these things were new. And you'll meet foundry workers, machinists, steam-shovel operators, farmers, all kinds of mechanics, and builders and working people. Just where are all these things hiding in a library, of all places? On the pages full of drawings and photographs in hundreds of books and magazines, of course.

Magazines are an easy first step into the world of old work. Americans have always been fascinated by technology. And for almost as long as there have been magazines in America there have been magazines about science and technology for general readers. There's no way to find exactly what you're looking for in a pile of century-old magazines, but that's the fun of library archaeology.

Old copies of *Scientific American* are a good place to start. The first issue came out in 1845 and, in those days, it was subtitled *An Illustrated Journal of Art, Science and Mechanics*. Don't worry about where to start. Just browse through a few copies and you'll find pages and pages of drawings of "new" machine tools, dynamos, water turbines, farm machinery, pumps, ships, surgical instruments, carriages, microscopes, everything imaginable (and some things that aren't). The main branch of a big-city library and nearby university libraries may also have copies of *American Mechanics Magazine* and the *Journal of the Franklin Institute* that go all the way back to the days when the Erie Canal was under construction and Oliver Evans was experimenting with steam engines. You'll find short, readable articles on technology in this century in two magazines that have been on the newsstands for years now, *Mechanics Illustrated* and *Popular Mechanics*.

Many occupations, trades, and crafts have had their own magazines. They are called "trade journals," and, over the years, there have been hundreds of them. It'll take you years of page turning to get through all the detailed illustrations and descriptions of work in *Railways Times, Farmer and Mechanic, Railway Age Gazette, American Machinist, Railroad Journal, Engineering News Record,* and *American Engineer.* It was in journals like these that I found many of the illustrations for this book. They're not easy to find, and even large libraries may have only a few issues of one or two. Trade journals are for the more advanced library archaeologist.

Hobby magazines haven't been around quite so long, but the history in them goes way back. *Model Railroader,* for one, always has pictures and plans for building old locomotives, bridges, tunnels, stations, warehouses and factories, trackside buildings, anything that was once a part of real railroading. Every issue of *Trains* magazine is another visit to a railroad in days passed. *Model Engineer,* a magazine from England (which makes it harder to find), is filled with articles, drawings, and photographs showing how to build and operate miniatures of historical steam engines and locomotives that run on "live steam." Ship model and model airplane builders have their own magazines filled with the lore and history of early sailing ships and aircraft. But you'll have to watch out. There are step-by-step instructions in all these magazines for building history in miniature and, before you know it, you'll be at work.

To find these magazines the librarian will have to dig pretty deep in some dusty, dimly lit shelves. If you look at the last date stamped into the book you'll see why; you're the first reader to check them out in thirty years! (I checked out a magazine that helped me write this book that was last checked out in 1928.) But you won't have much trouble if you use the card catalog.

If you know the title of a book or magazine, like one of the magazines I mentioned, look in the Author-Title catalog. But if you want to see what your library has on a certain subject, start with the Subject catalog. In this catalog subjects are listed alphabetically. Here will be listed magazines, books, trade journals, even photographic collections under subjects like:

Aqueducts	Dams	Gears
Bridges	Electric generators	Hoisting machinery
Canals	Farm buildings	Industrial buildings

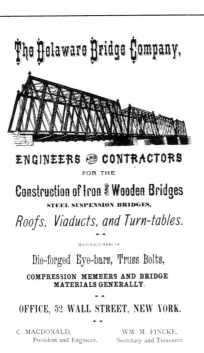

When you've found an interesting magazine, write down the title and the call number and—if it's not shown on the card—ask the librarian for the first volume. Many libraries have old magazines copied on film called microfiche. That's the beginning of another adventure, learning to use the reader. Most likely, you'll be handed a huge, dusty bound volume of yellowed magazines. Handle them very carefully. Old magazines get crispy and crunchy with age.

Enjoy your rainy day visit to a foundry in the 1870s or a farm where the wheat is threshed by steam, and don't forget to look at the ads.

Acknowledgements

This page is for me to say thank you to the friends who, in helping with the book, made the writing all the more enjoyable. Mark Rawitsch and Sandra Metzler-Smith of the Mendocino County Museum have been thoughtful teachers as well as friends, have given me a working knowledge of historical archaeology and invited me along to share with them some first-hand experiences in the field. Alicia Stamm, James Callahan, Eric DeLony, Mary Ison, and Nancy Roberts made it possible for me to reach across the miles and find the photographs and drawings I wanted in the collections of the Historic American Building Survey, the Historic American Engineering Record, and the Library of Congress. Tom Hahn of the American Canal Society, John Lamb of the Illinois Canal Society, James Brittain at the Georgia Institute of Technology, and Larry Lankton at Michigan Technological University helped me to find illustrations, too, each coming up with just the right images from their own personal collections and research. And when I had questions about railroads, John Witherbee of the Union Pacific always responded with useful answers and dozens of splendid locomotive photos. There are many others, and my thanks to them goes with the recognition of their work in the credits below.

Illustration Credits

American Canal Society—16; Wm. Edmund Barrett—ix (left, below), xi (right, above), 12, 98; Jack E. Boucher—vii, viii (left, above), xii, 20, 76, 96; James E. Brittain—14, 48; from Terrell Croft, *Steam-Engine Principles and Practice* (New York: McGraw-Hill, 1939)—37, 41; from George L. Fowler, *Forney's Catechism of the Locomotive* (New York: Railway Age, 1911)—72–73; Historic American Engineering Record—xiv, 4, 5, 7, 8, 11, 50, 51, 78, 79; Illinois Canal Society—16; Library of Congress—54, 55, 102; Jet Lowe—xiii; Mamod 80 Limited—40; National Museum of American History, Smithsonian Institution—28, 29, 32; National Park Service—vi; Ohio Historical Society—47; Myron B. Sharp and William H. Thomas—46; Union Pacific Railroad—x (left, above), 64–65; Utah Heritage Foundation—52; Robert M. Vogel—viii (below), 44.

Index